Praise for Grandparenting:

"Grandparenting: Renew, Relive, Rejoice is a wonderful reminder of how profound, life-changing, and fun becoming a grannie or a pop is. Reading about the experiences of Glamm, Popo, Nona, Grampy, Bubbie, etc.—along with helpful hints and advice—is a lovely way to learn about and deepen the pleasure of being with our grandchildren."

Lesley Stahl
60 Minutes, Author of *Becoming Grandma*

"The interesting thing about Grandparenting: Renew, Relive, Rejoice is not only that you learn a lot about your grandkids, but also, you learn a lot about yourself."

Bob Newhart
Comedian

"Becoming a grandmother (they call me Sassy) has exceeded, and then some, my wildest expectations. I love what this book offers. It is an incredible resource for anyone embarking on the grandparent journey."

Susan K. Feldman
Founder Get In The Groove, Co-founder One Kings Lane

"Walking through the pages with our grandchildren is a mutually beneficial journey as we encourage the conversation, contemplation and examination of the thoughts, feelings, and wisdom that is shared so clearly, thoughtfully, and beautifully in this book. I, for one, rejoice in the gift of its publication!"

Reveta Bowers
President, Common Sense Media National Board; Retired Head of School, The Center for Early Education

"A must read. You will never be more amazed as to how truly the old adage 'stop and smell the roses' applies. This book offers real-life activities with an understanding of how mindfulness elevates the cherished grandparent-grandchild relationship. You will definitely want to start practicing a more mindful approach to grandparenting."

Kay Ziplow
Co-founder Grandparentslink.com

"Offers just the right size bites for any nana, grandpa, grammie or papa. Whether to enhance your connections with your grandchildren, or to share the complexities of your role, this book by Siegel and Zinberg is filled with pearls of grandparenting wisdom."

Betsy Brown Braun
Child Development and Behavior Specialist, Author of *Just Tell Me What to Say* and *You're Not the Boss of Me*

"A wonderful book! Siegel and Zinberg offer readers tools to savor precious moments spent with grandkids. As we learn to pay attention, without judgment, this book sets the stage for a new way to focus in all aspects of daily life. As a pediatrician of 42 years, and the grandfather of nine small grandchildren, this book has enhanced the joy I feel as a more focused, less judgmental grandfather."

Andrew M. Matthew, MD, FAAP

"A gift to all grandparents . . . and to their grandchildren. It is smart, accessible, and really teaches us what mindfulness is in a practical way, full of useful ideas on how to make the most of the precious time we have with the grandchildren we love so much. I loved every page. I'm buying one for all of my friends who are grandparents."

Marlene Canter
Former LAUSD School Board President, Chaplin, Educator, Parent, Grandparent

"Kudos to Pam Siegel and Leslie Zinberg: these two authors used mindfulness as an important way to connect with children and teens. They emphasized the fact that, regardless of age, we all have the ability to grow with our grandchildren. This book is filled with sage advice, fabulous quotes, whimsical colorful drawings, and meaningful self-disclosure. There are numerous anecdotes that facilitate the reader capturing every point along the way. This book is a MUST READ for every grandparent who will be so happy to experience the support and the caring of two exceptional authors!"

Barbara K. Polland, PhD, LMFT
Professor Emeritus, California State University, Northridge, Child and Adolescent Development, Psychotherapist and Speaker, Author of *No Directions on the Package, Questions and Answers for Parents with Children from Birth to Age 12* and *We Can Work It Out—Conflict Resolution for Children*

"Grandparents are known for the many (sometimes too many) gifts that they lavish upon their grandkids. Most are gone and forgotten quickly. What if there was one gift you could give to yourself and your grandkids that would serve you both for the rest of your lives and provide a lasting bond? This book provides a path to the practice of mindfulness and opens the reader to a life well lived from the inside out. If you truly want to leave a legacy, make this book the cornerstone of your grandparent toolbox."

Christine Crosby
Editorial Director *GRAND* Magazine

"For any grandparent interested in deepening their relationship with their grandchildren, this book delivers. Inspirational, thought-provoking, and a joy to read."

Susan Stiffelman, MFT
Author *Parenting Without Power Struggles* and *Parenting with Presence*

Grandparenting
Renew, Relive, Rejoice
52 Ways to Mindfully Connect and Grow with your Grandkids
by Pam Siegel and Leslie Zinberg

© Copyright 2019 Pam Siegel and Leslie Zinberg

ISBN 978-1-63393-958-5

Published by

◤ köehlerbooks™

210 60th Street
Virginia Beach, VA 23451
800–435–4811
www.koehlerbooks.com

PAM SIEGEL   LESLIE ZINBERG

Grandparenting

RENEW, RELIVE, REJOICE

52 WAYS
to Mindfully Connect and Grow with Your Grandkids

VIRGINIA BEACH
CAPE CHARLES

WE DEDICATE THIS BOOK TO:

Our inspiring grandchildren
DYLAN
LILY
ETHAN
JACK
ASHER
SPENCER
GAVIN

Our wonderful children
JAMIE & JUDD ZINBERG
RODD ZINBERG
AMY & ADAM SIEGEL
SARA & JUSTIN ROSS

Our supportive and loving husbands
MICHAEL ZINBERG & LENNY SIEGEL

"The greatest gift we can make to others
is our true presence."
Thich Nhat Hanh

CONTENTS

Hold on to this book! If you are browsing through *Grandparenting: Renew, Relive, Rejoice*, you are probably involved in that very special relationship called grandparenting, or are aware of the power of mindfulness in relationships, or both. Authors Pam and Leslie have created a simple yet very powerful toolbox of 52 ideas and mindfulness-generating activities for grandparents and grandchildren to enjoy together. In this way, *Grandparenting: Renew, Relive, Rejoice* is a source for introducing mindfulness into your family.

As a mindfulness teacher and mentor, and a licensed marriage and family therapist for over twenty years, I have taught mindfulness to thousands of people in classes, retreats and therapy. During this time, interest in mindfulness has grown exponentially, beginning with people who were "meditators," and then eventually expanding in many directions, including medicine, psychology, education, and ultimately, and perhaps best, into the lives of everyday people. In working with my students and clients, I've had the privilege to witness, and come to more deeply understand, the ways people effectively use mindfulness in their daily lives. Through this mutual process of learning and growing together, one of the things that has become abundantly clear is if mindfulness is not presented in a down-to-earth, user-friendly, and practical way, then it is not accessible to most people.

Grandparenting: Renew, Relive, Rejoice has this easy, common-sense approach. It makes mindfulness understandable to grandparents, who will then teach it to their grandchildren—a little at a time, with simple and fun things to do together. The range of activities invites adults and children to relax together, connect, and bring mindfulness—a deliberate, kind awareness—

into the moment-to-moment experiences of mind, body and spirit. *Grandparenting: Renew, Relive, Rejoice* can deepen the special bond that grandparents and grandchildren already have, and show them ways to extend this loving awareness to others, nature, and the community.

By enjoying these activities together with a calm, open attention, some of the best aspects of physical and emotional well-being and emotional intelligence can be cultivated: learning to relax, and being attentive as well as noticing and identifying feelings, senses and thoughts. Additionally, important relationship qualities can grow through these experiences, such as being curious about others, developing a kind awareness of differences, being receptive, listening, laughing and being playful together, among many others.

It is exciting to see the abundance of research supporting the use of mindfulness for children, and watching these studies grow into creative, formal mindfulness curricula for students of all ages. In addition to these wonderful formal programs, there is also the need for the type of mindfulness practices found within *Grandparenting: Renew, Relive, Rejoice*. The activities in this book are down-to-earth invitations yet powerful reminders to see each moment of everyday life as a gift in which everyone involved can learn and grow.

I encourage you to approach these experiences with an open mind and heart, and a little curiosity. If you give it a chance, you might be surprised where this process takes you. Blessings on the journey of mindfulness, and enjoy!

Jerome Front, LMFT

When we became grandparents, we had no idea what to expect. We had a vision of what we thought grandparenting would look like—have fun, say yes to everything, and then, of course, at the end of the day, hand the kids back to their parents. However, we now know grandparenting is so much more.

Like us, many grandparents today are involved in the day-to-day care of grandchildren. As a result of dual-career and single-parent families, our adult children depend on us to help them navigate their fast-paced lives. We carpool to school and other activities, help with homework, and, if necessary, step in to handle discipline issues. At the same time, we must keep our comments to ourselves, especially when our grown children's wishes and rules differ from our own. This can be tricky.

The impetus for writing *Grandparenting: Renew, Relive, Rejoice* is to help grandparents manage these joyful, and sometimes complex, issues in a more "mindful" way. Mindfulness has taught us that it's not about spoiling our grandchildren; instead, it's about showing up and modeling good values. It's focusing on "presence above presents."

We asked a variety of grandparents to share their favorite anecdotes about being mindful with their grandchildren. These funny, poignant, heartfelt stories accompany the 52 moments of hands-on activities and games, thought-provoking quotes, and simple meditations.

Grandparenting: Renew, Relive, Rejoice helps grandparents and grandchildren effectively and lovingly relate and operate in the present together. These moments can be practiced in several different ways; for example, concentrate on one of the moments that addresses a specific need for you or your grandchild, such as "Prepare for Sleep" when dealing with challenges at bedtime.

Or select a moment that you think will be of particular interest to your grandchild, like "Enjoy Nature," or "Practice Yoga." Or jump around to a different page, and pick whatever speaks to you at the present time. Some moments are better suited for younger children, like "Breathe with the Bear," while others are more appropriate for older children, such as "Take a Break from Your Cell." You may want to practice one moment at a time by yourself before engaging your grandchildren. Perfection is not required; go at your own speed.

Keep *Grandparenting: Renew, Relive, Rejoice* at your bedside. Make it a habit to bring mindfulness into your daily life and the lives of your grandchildren.

M indfulness is paying attention to what is happening in the present moment, just as it is, without judgment. Sounds easy to do, but in fact it takes patience and practice. The easiest way to be present is to focus on the breath; it is our "friend" and regulator, easily accessible, and always with us.

Mindfulness can be practiced informally or formally, and both versions are demonstrated in our book. Formal mindfulness practice involves setting aside a specific amount of time to consciously "go inside" and be aware of what is sensed or felt in the body, using the breath as an anchor. This practice can include a sitting/walking meditation, body scan (systematic scan of body parts), or yoga session. Informal mindfulness involves finding brief moments in everyday life to be present. Instead of multitasking or spending extended periods on automatic pilot, the focus is on one activity at a time, without distraction.

Featured throughout the 52 moments in this book are nine overlapping concepts that form the foundation of mindfulness. They are:

BEGINNER'S MIND: Seeing afresh; looking at things as if for the first time, with an unbiased view and a sense of curiosity.

NON-JUDGING: Learning to be an impartial witness to our own daily experiences; not labeling them either good or bad, but just taking note of what they are now.

PATIENCE: Understanding and accepting that things often unfold in their own time, or being open to each moment in the present.

TRUST: Believing in our own instincts.

NON-STRIVING: Being in a state of non-doing and allowing ourselves to "be" without trying to change anything.

LETTING GO: Accepting things as they are with no attachment or expectation.

KINDNESS: Bringing compassion to ourselves in the moment, without self-blame or criticism.

ACCEPTANCE: Coming to terms with what is and seeing things as they really are in the present.

CURIOSITY: Connecting with senses and wanting to discover something new; asking questions about topics you do not know.

52 MOMENTS

GROWING YOUR SELF
Begin Anew
Slow Down
Do One Thing at a Time
Trust Yourself
Let Go of Judgments
Practice Patience
Invite Curiosity
Let Go
Set an Intention
Accept Yourself
Shed Inhibitions
Be Where You Are
Stay Current With Technology

RESPECTING OTHERS
Be Grateful
Engage in "Metta"
Respond Rather Than React
Practice Compassion
Accept What Is
Respect Silence
Forgive
Honor Uniqueness
Focus on the Positive
Mind Your Manners
Be Responsible
Take a Break from Your Cell
Honor Your Community and the Earth

TUNING IN TO YOUR BODY
  Smile
  Walk
  Listen
  Speak Mindfully
  See
  Smell
  Taste
  Touch
  Mindfully Eat
  Acknowledge Hunger and Fullness
  Scan Your Body
  Appreciate Your Body
  Prepare For Sleep

EXPERIENCING THE PRESENT MOMENT
  Observe Thoughts, Anger, and Worries
  Fall Awake
  Listen to the Bell
  Pause . . . a . . . Moment (PAM)
  Take Pleasure in Nature
  Laugh Out Loud
  Enjoy the Ride
  Practice Yoga

MEDITATIONS
  Calm Yourself
  S . . . T . . . O . . . P . . . Meditation
  Anchor Meditation
  Practice Square Breathing/Belly Breathing
  Breathe with the Bear

GROWING YOUR SELF

"Being a grandmother is truly one of life's greatest joys. And having two of your grandchildren living with you is an amazing experience, most of the time! As we all know, grocery shopping is NOT one of life's greatest activities, and going four times a week is quite a chore. But when you arrive home and your two-and-a-half-year-old grandson greets you at the door and exclaims, 'Grandma, what did you bring me today?' you can't help but smile from ear to ear. He grabs the bags and drags them into the kitchen with great enthusiasm, anticipating the treasures he will find. He pulls out one item at a time, yelling for joy, 'Chips, Grandma! Are these for me? Look, Grandma, apples . . . and some more bananas!' When he comes across an item he's not familiar with, he screams even louder, 'Grandma, look at this! What is it?' Then, when you tell him, with equal excitement he yells, 'Scallions, Grandma!' This precious little boy has turned grocery shopping into the best part of my day, and has taught me to find joy in the simple routines of daily life."
~ Grandma

Begin Anew

"In the beginner's mind there are many possibilities,
but in the expert's there are few."
Shunryu Suzuki

Children naturally possess innocence, wonder, and curiosity, as they see things for the first time without bias or preconceived ideas. This is "beginner's mind." Our grandchildren can teach us to recognize the extraordinary in the ordinary, see things afresh without expectation, and value the richness of each unique moment and experience.

With younger children, beginner's mind is more apparent. Watch their exuberance and amazement as they react to the color, size, and sound of a fire truck racing by, the enormity of a giraffe at the zoo, or their first time at any new activity.

Older children are beginning to form their own biases, yet still possess innate curiosity. Their beginner's mind may not be as visible as when they were younger; however, they still exude excitement and awe when seeing things for the first time. We need to encourage them to delve deeper into their reactions and thoughts. And, of course, answer the multitude of questions as they surface.

There is so much to learn from the grandchildren in our lives, whether they are young or grown-up. Let's slow down, breathe, and allow ourselves to be inspired by them.

"One purely magnificent moment occurred from something so simple. I was lying on the grass with my then four-year-old granddaughter, Charlotte, looking up at the sky and chatting about the cloud formations. 'What do you see, Grandy?' she asked. I replied, 'I see tufts of cotton balls.' (I'm not very creative). When I asked Charlotte what she saw, she went into a dreamy description of how the clouds seemed happy floating and bouncing around with no destination in mind. It was not necessarily profound (unless you're her Grandy, who thinks everything she says is remarkable); but, as she was talking, I glanced over at her and saw her look of total peace and contentment. She had me all to herself, neither of us rushing off. We talked about how wonderful it is to have 'spare time,' not always having to be busy. And then we talked about her friend and on and on, just lying there looking at the sky, our arms folded behind our heads, being spontaneous. It was pure joy." ~ Grandy

SLOW DOWN

"Slow down, calm down, don't worry, don't hurry,
trust the process."
Alexandra Stoddard

Too often we rush from one activity to another with our grandchildren, exclaiming, "Come on, look at the time!" What kind of message are we sending? Are we causing anxiety for them and for us as we hurry them along? Will it really matter if we're a few minutes late? Children operate at their own uninterrupted speed, and it's our job to understand where they are and where we are, in the current moment. We need to slow down and be mindful of the situation.

When it's time to leave an activity, allow enough time to make a smooth, peaceful exit. Younger children like to dawdle and need the time to transition as they move through their day. A five-minute warning does wonders. You may even want to set a timer on your phone (that way you're not the bad guy), and let them see the minutes count down. The goal is to avoid a meltdown.

As older children begin to assert their independence, we, as grandparents, need to pay attention to their desires and allow them to move at their own pace, within limits. Discuss the plan and time frame of the day so the kids know exactly when and what to expect. The five-minute warning is also a good option.

Remember, it's important to give children (and grandparents) free time to explore, relax, play, and treasure the moments.

"I cherish sleepovers with my grandkids because Pop and I get the kids all to ourselves and can smother them with love and nonstop attention. Each time they come over, we have a tradition. We say, 'Hey, kids, wanna have a party?' and of course they throw their arms around us and say, 'Yes!' We take a couple of apples, peel them, cut them in slices, and exclaim, 'Okay, we're ready.' We all jump into our bed and eat the apple slices. That's the party, pure and simple, just as Nana Jan did with me, and my mom, Nana Patty, did with our sons. These memories last a lifetime! What do my darling grandchildren say to us as they climb on Pop and me and squeeze us? They shout, 'We love you to the moon and back!' No feeling is better." ~ Nana & Pop

DO ONE THING AT A TIME

"Focus on one thing at a time. Enjoy it, taking the most pleasant memories of it into the next experience."
Unknown

What do you like to do with your grandchildren? Whatever it is, immerse yourself with patience and loving attention. Concentrate on one activity at a time—no multitasking. Let go of distractions and focus on being together. Playing a board game is a perfect way to demonstrate this idea:

⭐ Find a quiet place and turn off all phones and media.

⭐ Carefully read and follow the instructions with the help of your grandchildren.

⭐ Talk about strategy and good-natured competition.

⭐ Engage in open conversation.

⭐ Be enthusiastic. Get into it!

It doesn't matter what you do or how you spend time together; it's about being present and focused. Undoubtedly, this builds a stronger bond between you and your grandchildren.

"Recently my eight-year-old granddaughter arrived at my home to spend the afternoon while her brother went to another activity. She arrived with her box of markers and a brand-new recipe book proudly tucked under her arm. She ran straight to the room she occupies when in our home and returned with a pile of clean paper to announce that she was going to work on 'advertising posters for the new business I am opening with my best friend.' She gleefully exclaimed that she was opening a bakery that would make beautiful and delicious cookies, cakes, and donuts, and it would be called 'The Unicorn Bakery.' When I asked why she had decided to open a bakery, she replied, 'Because I am so good at baking things, and I always have such a good time baking at home with Mommy and with you here. And,' she continued, 'we can make money now and when I grow up!' Hearing her response, I was reminded that the fun times we have baking have given her both the skills and confidence to want to do some meaningful work, and they've also helped her to make the connection that 'work' that gives her joy now can perhaps support and give her satisfaction in the future." ~ Nana

TRUST YOURSELF

"I've learned that whenever I decide to trust something with an open heart, I usually make the right decision."
Maya Angelou

By coaching our grandchildren to think for themselves and trust their instincts, we empower them to make good decisions. This adds to their self-esteem and creates the belief that they are valuable, capable, and trustworthy individuals. Here are some suggestions to help build these qualities:

⭐ Ask their opinions.

⭐ Listen to them. Really listen.

⭐ Be interested in them—their thoughts, beliefs, or favorite hobbies/interests.

⭐ Give positive feedback, and do not criticize or make fun of their ideas or inquiries.

⭐ Give them choices. It's best to give younger children a limited number of options. For example, when asking what they would like to eat, or what they might want to wear, ask, "Grilled cheese or pasta, blue shorts or red shorts?"

⭐ Encourage self-expression and open conversation. This is most important with older children.

"Going to the bookstore is one of my favorite things to do with my grandchildren, ages ten and twelve. The last time we went, the man helping us was covered with tattoos from head to toe and had two nose piercings. I could feel my initial disapproval of him percolating, but my grandchildren were nonplussed about the way he looked. Being an open-minded liberal who strives to be nonjudgmental, I wanted to make sure I did not put my inner feelings on display. As it turns out, this guy's knowledge of books was exceptional. Plus, he was kind and had a great sense of humor. As I've learned—'you can't judge a book by its cover.'" ~ Gampop

"If you judge people, you have no time to love them."
Mother Teresa

Teaching our grandchildren to be less judgmental starts with us. We need to lead by example and show our grandchildren with actions and words that we accept people for who they are.

Here are a few tips on how to nurture open-minded grandchildren:

Read books about different cultures, religions, ethnicities, sexual orientations, appearances, and disabilities.

Discuss feelings that surface as they see people in various walks of life, e.g., the homeless man on the corner, or a child with special needs in their class.

Verbalize that it is okay to be different or unique; encourage individuality and inner confidence.

Use nonjudgmental language and keep negative, biased comments in check.

Conversations can vary according to the age of your grandchildren. As the kids mature, the dialogue will probably become more thoughtful and challenging.

"Since I spend a lot of time with my grandkids, I realize not every day is perfect, nor is my patience level. If a day begins bumpy, or we hit a rough spot, we take a deep breath and gather our patience. We walk backwards, go backwards up the stairs, read a book backwards, sing a song backwards—whatever it takes to hit the 'restart button.' We get pretty silly, and the bumps and impatience seem to disappear with the laughter." ~ Savta

"My granddaughter Sophie, age six, spends at least two nights a week at our house, since both her parents work night-shift jobs. I also work and time is limited, but I seem to have more patience with her than I did with my own daughter. We love cooking together, but it drives me a little bit crazy when Sophie takes her time gathering the ingredients for our favorite Romanian dishes and methodically organizes them as we prepare to cook. I have had to learn to slow down, take deep breaths, and realize it is more important to spend time with her than to be a speed demon in the kitchen." ~ Grandma G

PRACTICE PATIENCE

"A moment of patience, in a moment of anger,
saves a thousand moments of regret."
Unknown

At any age, grandchildren's temper tantrums, whining, eye-rolling, and not listening can be challenging for everyone, let alone the grandparents. Doing homework or not getting their way often results in struggle and resistance. Train your patience muscle by practicing these techniques:

FOR YOURSELF:
⭐ Slow down, access your breath, count to ten.

⭐ Think about what you are doing and feeling. Decide how to proceed. Pick your battles carefully.

FOR YOUNGER CHILDREN:
⭐ Distract them by diverting their attention to something other than the struggle at hand. Create silly lyrics to a favorite tune like "Rain Rain Go Away" and sing, "Whine Whine Go Away."

⭐ Use humor to lighten demanding moments.

FOR OLDER CHILDREN:
⭐ Respond calmly and respectfully. Listen carefully and validate their thoughts. Talk about their feelings.

⭐ Be clear and consistent with the consequences you impose on their challenging behavior.

⭐ Add humor when appropriate.

"While baking cookies with my four granddaughters, we got into a discussion of 'Where did I come from?' This was not the talk about where babies come from, but a discussion about their heritage. We pulled out a map and looked at the countries of their origins—Poland, Russia and France. We told them stories about the family we knew, including their grandparents and great-grandparents, and about some of the relatives we had never met. We discussed being a 'link in the chain' of our family and the importance of maintaining traditions. At the end of this wonderful discussion, my youngest granddaughter said, 'I am only one person. How can I come from so many places?' That was a brilliant question!" ~ Nami

"Our grandchildren look forward to treasure hunts at our house. Before the kids arrive, we bury a treasure and make an antique-looking map (signed by Captain Crunch), stained with tea and burnt at the edges. Dressed in their eye patches and kerchiefs, and equipped with compasses, pirate swords, and plastic shovels, the kids study the map and set off to find the treasure. Their curiosity is piqued, and they can't wait to find the stash." ~ Didi and Papa

INVITE CURIOSITY

"You can grow ideas in the garden of your mind."
Fred Rogers

Kids are naturally inquisitive. They want to know everything, and they want to know it NOW! Here's how to cultivate a curious mind for you and your grandchildren:

⭐ Stimulate discussion with interest and enthusiasm by asking questions. Emphasize that there is no such thing as an unintelligent question or idea.

⭐ Pretend to be detectives. Look up information together on the Internet and at the library when you want to delve deeper into a particular topic. Promote free play and unstructured exploration at every age.

⭐ Encourage passion for a particular hobby, sport, or interest. Read books on a favorite subject, get tickets to sporting events, attend music or dance concerts, visit museums, and go to plays. Stay involved.

⭐ Include discussions about your own personal experiences and interests. Kids love to hear your stories, especially the times you may have gotten into trouble, or overcame adversity.

⭐ Support independent thinking, especially with older children. Always ask them what they think and stress that their ideas matter.

"My granddaughter lives 5,000 miles away in London. I live in Southern California. In the early days, when we Skyped, which we used to do more frequently before she 'grew up,' (she's now six), I knew that if I wanted to get and hold her attention, I was going to have to be silly. I became 'naughty' Grandpa, using inflated facial expressions and verbal exaggerations, saying things that slightly broke Mommy's rules. This made us secret allies and served to make a toddler who didn't know me except as a screen presence named Opa, real. By the way, she loved to report our interactions to her mom, who joined in with mock outrage. I wanted to be in my granddaughter's life, but more to the point, I wanted her to want me to be in her life. Her mother—my daughter—and her father had broken up, so I wanted her to know there was one man in her life that she wasn't going to see only on weekends. She knows I love her unconditionally. You know how I know? Two weeks ago she asked me to be her pen pal. These days, when we Skype, she doesn't always want to speak. I hang back, like a guest over for a cup of tea, and I don't push it. Sometimes I'll ask her a question, and if she answers, great. Sometimes she doesn't answer, and that's okay. At least she knows I'm there." ~ Opa

LET GO

"Learning to let go, this is the secret to happiness."
Buddha

When our children or grandchildren do things we don't like, or there is a situation that doesn't make us happy, can we "let go" of our judgments and anger? Mindfulness teaches us to keep an open mind and not be attached to our emotions, opinions, rituals, and ideas. This is easier said than done, but here are some tools for both grandchildren and grandparents when things don't go the way we want:

⭐ Breathe. Count to ten. Center yourself.

⭐ Take a walk to clear your mind and remove yourself from a difficult situation.

⭐ Call a friend or coworker who normally offers opinions you respect.

⭐ Be rational. Use your mind to help you assess the positive and negative aspects of the situation.

⭐ Make a decision not to attach to negative feelings. Anger is hard on our bodies and our souls.

⭐ Add humor to lighten the mood. Don't sweat the small stuff.

⭐ If we, as grown-ups, learn to "let go," our grandchildren will follow.

"When I was a little girl, my mom taught me her favorite dessert recipes. My three daughters tell me that one of their fondest childhood memories is of bedtime cookies straight from the oven. Now that my girls have families of their own, and my husband and I have 'sixty-something metabolisms,' I have no excuse to bake. That is, unless my grandkids come for a visit! My intention is to pass on this family tradition of baking and creating memories. The kids' favorite is a recipe I have perfected over the years— chocolate chip oatmeal coconut cookies. The kids stand on step stools, taking turns adding butter and sugar, then cracking the eggs into a clear glass bowl (so I can spot any bits of white shell). We sift, measure, and add the dry ingredients . . . then come the chocolate chips. The children position their stools to watch the cookies bake inside the lighted oven. Finally, as we sit at the kitchen table, savoring our warm cookies with ice-cold milk, I recount stories of baking with their moms at their age. I am mindful that if it weren't for my grandkids, I would have no reason to do one of my favorite things." ~ Grandma Sandy

SET AN INTENTION

*"When you set an intention, when you commit,
the entire universe conspires to make it happen."*
Sandy Forster

S etting a goal or intention is an amazing tool to help navigate many scenarios in life. It is a valuable way to change behavior and create memories.

⭐ Focus your attention on a specific situation or emotion. Mentally or verbally rehearse how you would like things to transpire. For example, "I will not raise my voice when my grandkids bicker," or "I will not worry about the mess in the kitchen when the grandkids come over and cook." Or set a mindful intention to be patient, nonjudgmental, or more present. Say to yourself, "I will only check my cell phone every hour," or "I will be more tolerant of other people's opinions," or "I will be more considerate with my spouse at dinner tonight."

⭐ Teach grandchildren of any age to set intentions by helping them make a plan for how they want to behave. Prior to playing any game, discuss the importance of cooperation and sharing, not winning or losing. Or talk about how to be a good host/friend before a visit. Or discuss the importance of good manners before sitting down in a restaurant.

⭐ Create situations with your grandchildren that instill ideals or beliefs that are important to you and that you would like to pass on to them. For example, hosting traditional holiday dinners, family game nights, Sunday barbecues, or any other custom that you value.

"I love doing projects with my grandchildren. One day, while teaching them how to draw self-portraits, one of my adorable grandsons said to me, 'Popo, you did a good job on your self-portrait, but you forgot something.' He took his marker and proceeded to carve three strong lines on my portrait. He said, 'You forgot to draw the lines on your forehead!' I laughed and said to him, 'You're right! I am so proud of those lines, because they show the world how well and how long I have lived. And when you grow up and have lines on your face, I want you to be proud of them, too.' He proceeded to say, 'You also have lines on your neck!' I smiled at him, nodded, and thought to myself, *You little s—!*" ~ Popo

"I make a point of letting my grandson know that I'm not perfect. Often times, I get distracted talking when I'm driving him home and forget to make the correct turn. He is always there to say, 'Glammy, you went the wrong way again.' I laugh and say, 'I'm so silly and very glad you're here to remind me.' One time he actually gave me directions to get home—he was four at the time!" ~ Glammy

ACCEPT YOURSELF

"Finally I am coming to the conclusion that my highest ambition is to be what I already am."
Thomas Merton

We are imperfect beings. At times, we can be forgetful, difficult, impatient, or self-centered. It's important to let our grandchildren see that we love and take pride in ourselves, despite our shortcomings and challenges of aging. Here are some ideas to inspire our grandchildren, and us, to love and accept ourselves:

Keep a sense of humor. "Silly Grandma misplaced her keys and glasses again" may be words the grandchildren hear over and over.

Focus on the positive. Verbalize self-affirmations like "I am happy with who I am," or "I like how I handled that situation," or "I am working on being a better friend."

Practice self-care with balanced meals, consistent exercise, and adequate rest.

Apologize when in the wrong—gracefully. Learn to lighten up and not make a big deal out of everything.

Resist negative self-talk, but at the same time acknowledge that we are not perfect beings. There is always room for improvement.

"Playing in our pretend band is my favorite way to connect with my four-and-a-half-year-old granddaughter and two-and-a-half-year-old grandson. I love music, and now so do they! We all have our instruments consisting of guitars, piano, harmonicas, drums, tambourines, and microphones. We even use pretend instruments like tennis rackets, ping pong paddles, and play golf clubs to make up instruments that we don't have. Collectively, we decide on songs to sing, then dance and play together as if we're a finely tuned group. We take turns being the lead singer, the lead guitarist, or the drummer. When we can't decide on a song, I encourage the kids to simply make up words or sounds and jump around. We have achieved so much playing time that I sometimes believe we're ready to go on the road. What we've really accomplished is some spectacular together time that is focused on just us, and the moment. The sessions are a place for all of us to let loose, but leave me needing a nap!"

~ G-pa

SHED INHIBITIONS

"Live, laugh, love."
Unknown

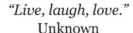

Watch children engage in make-believe play. They are full of energy, wonder, and enthusiasm as they live and fantasize in their own world. We need to let go of our self-consciousness and self-judgment, and join them in the pure joy and innocence of the present moment.

Get on the floor, connect, and have fun.

Dance, sing, improvise, and laugh with gusto. Put on music and bring out the instruments.

Dress up in costumes with your grandchildren. Play office, princess, superheroes, police, doctor or school.

Get outside and join in with bubbles, tag, hide-and-seek, sports, and whatever they love.

Step into their creative experience, connect with their playfulness, and bond.

"I love doing creative projects with my grandkids and cherish the focused time we spend together without distractions. One of our favorite things to do is sew. When my granddaughters were younger, they couldn't wait to come to my house and pick out pieces of colorful and textured fabric I had stored in a treasure trunk. They would take turns sitting on my lap at the sewing machine, and we'd sew together. We often made little purses with a strap to put over their shoulders. They would each fill their purses with a few buttons, a little mirror, one of my old lipsticks, or maybe even a quarter, and they would be so proud as they left for home. The girls are now older and still look forward to our special sewing time. Recently, I took them to see a Marc Chagall exhibit of the costumes he had designed and painted beautifully for *The Firebird* ballet. We then decided it would be fun to recreate the Chagall-like designs. I gave the girls white muslin cut into long petals and some fabric paint and let them create. They each sat at the sewing machine concentrating while they sewed their painted petals to a wide ribbon to tie around their waists like a skirt. We decorated them with glitter and rhinestones, and I attached some pink tulle to complete the fantasy. They were beautiful! These magical moments are priceless." ~Nonna

*"We have only now, only this single eternal moment opening
and unfolding before us, day and night."*
Jack Kornfield

Children are easily distracted and impatient to get to the next thing, and we are just as guilty of this. "Are we there yet?" is a question we hear over and over again from our grandchildren. Think about it. Often we are on autopilot. Next time your mind wanders or your grandchildren lose focus:

⭐ Pause and take a breath.

⭐ Bring your mind and your grandchildren's minds back to the present moment. Remind everyone to "be where they are."

⭐ Make positive comments about the minute-to-minute experience—the music on the radio, the scenery, being together, etc. When driving grandchildren, it's best not to vocalize how rushed and frantic you feel about getting to the next place.

⭐ Express with language and behavior that you are happy in what you are presently doing, and not worrying about what's in the future. Tell them, "I love being with you right here, right now."

"Being a grandparent is one of the great joys in my life, but being the out-of-town grandmother has its challenges. So, I have turned to technology to stay connected. When the kids were younger, my daughter would call from the car with my grandsons, Bryan and Jason, and they would talk to me 'on the radio.' Then came Skype, but when the younger boys, Ethan and Spencer, were toddlers, they didn't want to sit in front of a screen and would often hit the button disconnecting the call. A camera with a wide-angle lens mounted on the TV was the next solution, as it gave my husband and me a view of the kids running around doing somersaults and playing the guitar. Not wanting to be a talking head, I started reading books and talking to the kids with puppets. Sometimes I think they called just to talk to Gigi's puppets. I'm certainly no ventriloquist, but the boys never even noticed that my mouth was moving. It was such fun! Now that my grandsons are a little older, they prefer using FaceTime to connect with us. They know they can call us anytime, and we love it when they do! On one of my recent visits, my grandson's parting words were, 'Gigi, text me when your plane lands.' We've come a long way from being a voice on the car radio! Thank you, technology." ~ Gigi

STAY CURRENT WITH TECHNOLOGY

"It is not what technology does to us, it is what we do to technology. Get smart with technology, choose wisely and use it in a way that benefits both you and those around you."
Headspace.com

Technology is our grandchildren's day-to-day reality. We need to be fluent in their "tech" language in order to better connect with them. It is up to us to educate ourselves about the numerous choices, whether it's games, apps, websites, television programs, movies, texting, coding, Twitter, Snapchat, Instagram, or FaceTime. The options are mind-boggling. Here are some suggestions to become digitally savvy.

⭐ First and foremost, ask your grandchildren for help. They probably know more than you. Remember they have grown up with technology.

⭐ Do an online research project on a subject that interests your grandchildren. Work together to navigate the extensive media environment.

⭐ Learn how to text. Tweens and teens love this way of communicating.

⭐ Look at websites such as www.commensensemedia.org and www.parentpreviews.com for up-to-date guides on the best age-appropriate media selections.

RESPECTING OTHERS

"Gratitude and prayer come up a lot when life presents challenges for my grandchildren at school, in sports, or at home. I've told them to try and start or end each day thinking of three things to be grateful for. And to enjoy the simple pleasures in life—overflowing bubble baths, huge jigsaw puzzles at holiday time, massive sofa pillow and blanket forts, special closet hideaways, sparkling stickers and princess costumes, and their delight in helping to feed and walk my dog, Westie. While we've had special vacation times together, the everyday moments are the most gratifying." ~ Ama

BE GRATEFUL

"The single greatest thing you can do to change your life today would be to start being grateful for what you have right now. And the more grateful you are, the more you get."
Oprah Winfrey

How do we teach our grandchildren to understand and show gratitude? How do we teach them to be happy with what they have? Try these engaging activities:

⭐ Comment on what you are grateful for in front of your grandchildren, i.e. the food on the table, the gorgeous day, or the smiles on their faces.

⭐ Together with your grandchildren, write or draw three things you each are grateful for. These can be something meaningful like spending time with family or having good health, or something small like enjoying your favorite movie or meal.

⭐ Make a gratitude jar. Each time anyone expresses gratitude, add a penny. Who can accumulate the most pennies?

⭐ Keep a (free) gratitude app on your phone to remind you to be grateful every single day. Older children love this.

Watch the gratitude habit escalate. The more you appreciate what you have, the more content you feel.

"One of my biggest joys in life is picking up my grandson from school and taking him to karate. It is our date every Tuesday afternoon. Parking close to karate is always a challenge, and it is a topic of discussion for us every week. Only in LA would a six-year-old have knowledge and opinions about parking! A few months ago, after class was over, we came back to our car and saw a note attached to the windshield saying that money had been put in our meter because the time had expired. We couldn't believe our luck! After asking around, we found that a woman from the bank had done this for us. My grandson was amazed, as was I. We could not believe that someone was so thoughtful. This led us into a discussion about random acts of kindness and how it makes us want to do the same for others. This incident has had a definite impact on my grandson because he continually brings it up. We brainstorm about ways to 'pay it forward' and together have come up with a few ideas that he hopes to implement." ~ Gramps

ENGAGE IN "METTA"

"The greatest work that kindness does to others is that it makes them kind themselves."
Amelia Earhart

A "metta" (loving-kindness) meditation is a way to bring compassion to yourself and others. Older children may be better suited for this sophisticated meditation, due to their maturity level. Practice together with your grandchildren:

⭐ Find a comfortable place to sit, close your eyes, and begin to breathe, slowly and quietly.

⭐ Talk about what makes everyone feel good and puts a smile on each other's faces. It may be a loved one, a pet, a friend, a book, a hobby, a toy, or a game.

⭐ Place your hands over your chest and mentally concentrate on the warm feelings.

⭐ Imagine spreading these comforting thoughts to family and friends. What are you experiencing? Is your heart more open now?

⭐ Bring the positive feelings towards yourself. Do you feel your heart expand, your body tingle?

⭐ Discuss any thoughts or emotions that arise.

"My granddaughter has long, beautiful hair. Recently, she spent the night at our house, and in the morning, she washed her hair. We insisted that she dry it because it was a cold wintry day. She used a small round metal brush with bristles, wrapping her long strands around the brush so tightly that the hair was caught in the brush. The hair became so tangled that the strands would not release. It was frightening. We tried to untangle the hair, but it was hurting her and giving her a headache. She kept screaming, 'Just cut my hair!' The challenge was to keep all of us calm, and not have to cut her hair. Ultimately, we added gobs of conditioner and cut the bristles off the brush. We kept taking deep breaths (and so did she), while simultaneously talking her through the process, even trying to add a little humor. One hour later, with both of us working, the hair released. Whew! Patience and calm saved us." ~ Nana and Papa

RESPOND RATHER THAN REACT

"Respond from the center of the hurricane, rather than
reacting from the chaos of a storm."
George Mumford

Y ou may have found yourself "reacting" to a stressful situation with yelling or inappropriate language, instead of "responding" calmly. Later you realize you could have handled things differently. You're not alone. Next time, try this:

⭐ Breathe. Count to four as you inhale. Then count to four as you exhale.

⭐ Begin to slow down.

⭐ Think about what is happening right now.

⭐ Create a space between your feelings and your behavior.

⭐ Think again and decide how to proceed.

⭐ Do you feel calmer and more centered? Hopefully, pausing has given you more clarity on how to respond.

⭐ Now, respond.

This is a great tool to practice and teach your grandchildren, especially when you or they are having a meltdown.

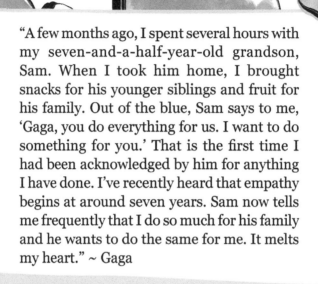

"A few months ago, I spent several hours with my seven-and-a-half-year-old grandson, Sam. When I took him home, I brought snacks for his younger siblings and fruit for his family. Out of the blue, Sam says to me, 'Gaga, you do everything for us. I want to do something for you.' That is the first time I had been acknowledged by him for anything I have done. I've recently heard that empathy begins at around seven years. Sam now tells me frequently that I do so much for his family and he wants to do the same for me. It melts my heart." ~ Gaga

"It was a Sunday night dinner and the whole family was together. Elisabeth, one of our three daughters, was making fun of me (as usual), and my granddaughter, Sadie, stopped her and said, 'Aunt Lizzy, when you make fun of GG (me), it hurts my feelings because GG and I are the same person.'" ~GG

"Education today needs not only to develop intelligence, but also to support basic human values of warm-heartedness and compassion."
Dalai Lama XIV

One of our roles are a grandparent is to help instill empathy into our grandchildren's lives, especially with the current political climate and the rise of bullying in schools. Here's how we can help develop the "compassion muscle" in our grandchildren:

⭐ Model consideration and appreciation.

⭐ Verbalize the value of compassion.

⭐ Resolve conflict with generosity of spirit.

⭐ Accept differences in others.

⭐ Do something special for a friend.

⭐ Take care of a pet.

⭐ Make someone feel better with a hug or a personal note.

⭐ Be charitable and volunteer your time.

⭐ Put yourself in someone else's shoes.

When we surround our grandchildren with compassion, we create a positive environment for them to emulate.

"Our daughter and her family live in New York with our three grandchildren, ages fifteen months to seven years. We live 3000 miles away. She and her husband have lived there for over twelve years, and we've had to adjust. It's certainly not an ideal situation, and there are times when we get sad and angry. But, overall, we have learned to accept the long distance as a reality. Most importantly, our daughter is very happy with her life and community of friends, and that makes us happy. We focus on the silver lining. Thank goodness for Facetime! We get to see our grandchildren doing their activities all week long, plus we make it a point to see them every two or three months. Just yesterday, we saw our older grandson on the zip line at summer camp and our youngest walking for the first time. We felt as though we were actually there!" ~ Grannie and Poppy

ACCEPT WHAT IS

"The moment you accept what troubles you've been given,
the door will open."
Rumi

It is not easy to let go of judgments and expectations, and "accept what is," especially when we are not pleased with a particular circumstance. We can choose to be miserable or upset, or adjust our attitude and be appreciative of what we have. Self-awareness combined with positive thinking leads to increased tolerance of challenging situations. For example:

⭐ When we disagree with our grown children's parenting or disciplining styles, remember we are the grandparents, not the parents. Stop, breathe, bite your tongue.

⭐ When dynamics with in-laws aren't perfect, stay calm, use good judgment, watch your words, and try to accept them for who they are. Keeping peace is a priority.

⭐ If we are unhappy about how infrequently we see our grandchildren, whether they live close by or far away, take a moment to appreciate any time spent together. Be happy with what you have.

⭐ When we notice that our kids and grandkids demonstrate values different from ours, whether they are socio-cultural, spiritual, familial, personal, material, or political, we must do our best to acknowledge and understand their perspective. Remember, it is their journey.

"Last month I took my two grandsons to a park. I wanted to have some outside time with them. This park has it all—airplanes for viewing, long walkways for scooting, nice trees and grass for sitting, and swings, slides, and a high tower for playing. We brought a picnic lunch and sat eating and watching everything. I saw the sheer fascination and focus on their beautiful faces as the planes took off and landed. At one point, there were no planes coming or going. We sat together not saying a word, just enjoying this quiet time and the beauty of nature." ~ Memaw

"Silence is the sleep that nourishes wisdom."
Francis Bacon

Many of us are uncomfortable with silence and feel as though we need to fill the space with words. While silence can feel awkward and foreign, it can also bring clarity and tranquility. Silence allows us to relax our minds, renew our spirit, and get in touch with our innermost feelings. Whether alone or with grandchildren, set aside a time to be silent.

FOR YOUNGER CHILDREN:

Create a "quiet area" that kids know is their safe, silent place. Fill it with pillows, coloring books, stickers, storybooks, or anything else to help them calm down and enjoy the stillness.

Play the "silence game" and see who can hang in the longest without uttering a sound.

FOR OLDER CHILDREN:

Discuss the value of silence.

Ask them how they find inner peace.

Play the "silence game." Most likely the responses will be different with the older kids versus the younger ones. Notice how the older set may be more self-conscious and prone to giggling. At the same time, the game could elicit a thoughtful discussion about how it feels when there is silence.

Invite them to a meal where no talking is allowed. Watch what happens during the silence. Does anyone feel uneasy, embarrassed—or content?

"A few months ago, I went to pick up my seven-year-old grandson from his house to take him to an activity. When I arrived at the house, there were more cars on the street than usual, so I parked at the end of their cul-de-sac in front of an unknown house. Later, when my grandson and I got into the car, we heard a loud knocking on my car window. Much to our surprise, an elderly man was standing there yelling at us about parking in front of his house. He was extremely angry because he had hired construction workers, and they had to work around my car. I felt my body begin to tense up, and a part of me wanted to yell back. I took a deep breath and realized how irrational this man was acting. I wanted to model a forgiving attitude in front of my grandson, who was sitting there with a shocked look on his face. With as much calm as I could muster, I apologized to the neighbor. After we drove away and numerous times since this interaction, my grandson and I have had meaningful discussions about forgiveness and how breathing can help you remain calm. What a great life lesson for us both!" ~ Grammy

FORGIVE

*"Remembering a wrong is like carrying
a burden on the mind."*
Buddha

Learning to forgive those who have disappointed us is not an easy task. Holding anger inside builds resentment and is physically disabling. Practice this loving-kindness meditation with your grandchildren to help you and them understand the concept of forgiveness:

⭐ First, bring to mind someone or something you love, either a family member, friend, or pet. Repeat the following words as you think about the person or animal: "May you be safe, may you be healthy, may you live with ease." Notice the positive feelings that arise.

⭐ Next, bring to mind someone who is difficult to forgive, such as a bully at school or work. Repeat the "May you be safe" meditation. See if you can lighten your reactions to this difficult person. Do you notice a shift in attitude as you say this meditation? Discuss what feelings surface. Has your anger shifted, or not?

This exercise is more appropriate for older children, but it is always interesting to see how kids of all ages respond. It may open a broader discussion about dealing with bullies or other difficult situations.

My grandson is a bright, articulate, and pensive five-and-a-half year-old. He plays on a seasonal basketball team outside of school. I went to see one of his games and I noticed two brothers on his team. One boy played very well and the other had difficulty running and walking. The boy that was challenged worked hard to keep up with the others. The opposing team had a small group of boys gathered, ready to begin the game. They were looking at the challenged boy and were making negative comments about him. My grandson ran up to the group of boys and spoke harshly: "Hey, stop talking about him. He is my friend and that is not nice." The mother of the boys was watching from the sidelines. After the game, she came over, praised my grandson, and told him he deserved an extra dessert at dinner for sticking up for his friend. He was so proud of himself. It was a win for everyone. ~ Gaga

HONOR UNIQUENESS

"Today you are you! That is truer than true!
There is no one alive who is you-er than you!"
Dr. Seuss

Not all children are the same; not all grandchildren are the same. We, as grandparents, need to appreciate and accept the varied abilities, personalities, interests, and temperaments of our grandchildren. While some kids can spend the whole day playing sports, others prefer art, reading, music, or computers. Some may have a disability or face a unique physical or mental challenge. Certain children may be shy, some dramatic, and others funny or loud. It is up to us to accept their differences and, at the same time, encourage our grandchildren to respect and celebrate uniqueness in themselves and others.

⭐ Do not compare your grandchildren to their siblings or any other kids. This is crucial.

⭐ Get involved in their unique hobbies or interests. If they love trains, research trains. If they love baseball, read up and discuss players with them; start a baseball card collection. If they love to sing or dance, take them to the theater or concerts.

⭐ Discuss tolerance, diversity, and disabilities. Help them embrace and understand differences in others.

⭐ Give them the message that we are all special in our own way and it is okay to be authentic.

⭐ Let them learn to be comfortable in their own skin.

"My third grandchild, Sasha, was born with Down Syndrome. I knew immediately that this little girl had been delivered to the right home with the perfect mom, dad, and sister to love her unconditionally with no judgment. The first week of Sasha's life was spent in the NICU. While she was in the hospital, we had the opportunity to learn more about Down Syndrome and to process and accept this special gift of life that had blessed our family. My son and daughter-in-law have taught us all to see the light in the darkness, embrace opportunity amidst the challenges, be present in the moment, and grateful for the new life we have been given. It's been almost two years since Sasha was born. She has brought more light and love into our family than we could have ever imagined. Sasha has taught us to accept the differences we see in each other, slow down, be positive, and appreciate the smallest successes in life. She has become our spiritual guide." ~ Baba

FOCUS ON THE POSITIVE

"We can complain because rose bushes have thorns, or rejoice because thorn bushes have roses."
Abraham Lincoln

Positive thinking can be a challenge because our brains are wired to focus on negativity. By being in the moment and acknowledging good things as they are happening, we become more optimistic, resilient and confident. We actually can change our brains and our lives, and those of our grandchildren . . . but it takes regular practice and commitment.

⭐ Discuss the phrase "every cloud has a silver lining." Explain there's a brighter side to difficult situations and there are ways to solve, learn, or accept them. For example, if your grandchildren are upset when they don't get picked for a team or the school play, validate their disappointment. At the same time, reframe the situation and point out a positive outcome: now they will have more time for other special activities or friends.

⭐ Place a half-full glass of water in front of your grandchildren and talk about the idea of half full versus half empty. This is a great exercise for older children.

⭐ Practice being cheerful and hopeful in life. At the dinner table, take turns naming three highlights of the day, focusing on the "roses" in life.

"So, I am at my desk in my office at the house, a private place, and in walks Dylan, my granddaughter. She's just turned eight. Beautiful and smart. She doesn't knock; she knows she's always welcome. She sits on the couch and says, 'Dinner is ready. Everybody is waiting downstairs.'

"I say, 'I'll be right down, in a moment.' She knows I'm working, and she respects that, so she waits a beat . . . and says, 'It's ready now.'

"I say, 'I'll be right down,' and throw her a kiss. Back to work.

"She sits a beat more and says, 'WE should go down.' I nod and mumble, 'Soon.'

"She waits, but does not move. A few seconds pass. Then . . . 'Are you ready?'

"'Just a . . . you know,' I say.

"Finally, she says, 'C'mon, GZ,' her name for me, 'Let's GO!'

"I turn and look at her beautiful face and she just smiles. I melt.

"'How come YOU got to be the one to come get me?'

"Her answer came without the slightest hesitation. 'Because they knew you'd blow everybody else off.'

"I took her hand and went right down." ~ GZ

MIND YOUR MANNERS

"Children are natural mimics who act like their parents despite every effort to teach them good manners."
Unknown

Good manners are a hot topic among grandparents. We expect our grandchildren to be polite and respectful of others. How do we help them do this?

⭐ Model good etiquette by saying "please," "thank you," "excuse me."

⭐ When your grandchildren forget to use their manners, gently ask, "Is there another way to say this?" or "Is there a word missing here?" or "What's the magic word?"

⭐ Prior to eating at home or at a restaurant, reiterate the rules of good table manners: no leaving the table without permission, running around, talking loudly, or using electronics.

⭐ Talk to your grandchildren about how to behave when meeting someone for the first time, such as acknowledging their presence with direct eye contact or a respectful greeting.

Learning manners can be a positive experience for our grandkids and for US! Keep it fun!

"Our six-year-old grandson Jack loves to build everything—Legos, Stem toys, magnetic tiles. Recently, he and my husband put together a portable rebound net in our backyard so Jack could throw softballs at the net and have them bounce back to him and refine his catching skills. What intrigued us was how Jack read the diagrams and figured out how to put the net together. He was totally responsible for calling out the directions, explaining how to assemble each part. He was so good at this that my husband even allowed him to use a hammer to tighten the net in the ground. Now, when he comes over, he automatically sets up and takes down the net without being asked. The more responsibility he is given, the more he rises to the occasion and the prouder he feels." ~ LeaLea

BE RESPONSIBLE

*"The willingness to accept responsibility for one's own life is
the source from which self-respect springs."*
Joan Didion

Being responsible grandparents is twofold. First, we need to examine ourselves and be accountable for our own words, actions, and behavior. Secondly, we need to teach our grandchildren to do the same.

FOR GRANDPARENTS:

★ Apologize when making a mistake. Be transparent and ready to discuss wrongdoings.

★ Follow through with promises—be true to your words. Do not blame others for your misbehavior.

★ Follow rules. No one is above the law. This is especially true when driving.

★ Model good work ethics.

★ Go out of your way to help family and friends in need. Volunteer in your community.

FOR GRANDCHILDREN:

★ Give them household chores like setting and clearing the table, helping with the dishes, or taking care of the household pet.

★ Teach them to clean up after themselves, such as putting away toys, clothes, and games.

★ Encourage them to follow your household rules, whatever they may be.

"When I am with my grandchildren, I try to see them for who they are and then relate to them in their own individual way. I insist on eye-to-eye contact when having a conversation or sitting down to eat. In fact, we recently had a family dinner and I realized just how much we are all addicted to our screens. I had prepared a delicious meal, and no one was paying attention to my creation. I got so frustrated that I ran and got a basket and insisted that everyone get rid of their phones while we ate so there were no more temptations. We ultimately had a delightful dinner filled with conversation and laughter. I really see how life without screens enhances my relationship with my grandchildren."
~GoGo

TAKE A BREAK FROM YOUR CELL

"Life is what happens when your cell phone is charging."
Unknown

Cell phones are a mixed blessing. They are addictive. The challenge is to use them in moderation. When you are with your grandchildren, spend uninterrupted time with them and notice how much more involved and connected you feel. Here are some tips on how to keep away the constant technology distractions:

✴ Place your cell phone out of sight to make sure you are truly present. Hide it if necessary. Or create a cell phone basket where phones temporarily live during special bonding time.

✴ Unplug from your cell phone, especially during mealtime and bedtime.

✴ Try not to take personal phone calls when in the car with your grandchildren.

✴ Look at texts and emails less frequently. For example, set a timer and check for messages every hour instead of every few minutes.

✴ See if you can use the phone only for emergencies. Good luck!

✴ Monitor usage of cell phone games. Do not use the phone as a babysitter.

"I've always thought of myself as a good citizen. That is, until my grandkids (ages six and ten) came along. They have made me more conscious of recycling, not littering, and 'going green.' If I dare have garbage in my hand and look like I am looking for a place to discard it, I am given a stern warning: 'You are not going to drop that on the street, are you?' Eco education is an important part of their elementary school curriculum and has taught them to be environmental advocates. During a drought, I had timers in my house, and if I exceeded the time by only a minute, there was a comment. I so appreciate what they have taught me and how much more eco-conscious I have become." ~ Grandpa Bill

HONOR YOUR COMMUNITY AND THE EARTH

"I hold the Earth and the Sky with love in my heart. I hold the Oceans and Rivers with love in my heart. I hold the creatures of the Earth with love in my heart. Beings big or small, near or far, living now, or to come. May they be happy, May they be safe, And may their hearts be filled with joy."
Joseph Emet

Are you mindfully aware of the environment? Do you recycle? Just as we respect ourselves, and others, we need to serve our community and honor the Earth. It is our job to take care of this planet so it is available for generations to come. With your grandchildren:

★ Participate in a local clean-up day or a recycling project.

★ Volunteer at a local food pantry, feed the homeless, or donate to the cause of your choice.

★ Demonstrate water conservation. Set timers for showers and baths.

★ Plant a vegetable garden to teach the concept of "farm to table."

★ Work together to better our world.

Go green!

TUNING IN TO YOUR BODY

"One of the most touching moments at this stage of life is such a simple and poignant one for me. My granddaughter, Allison, was sitting next to me on the sofa. She lovingly took my hand and started feeling my thin, aging skin and gently pulling it and running her finger over the pronounced veins. Without a word being said, our eyes met, and the moment captured everything . . . how I was changing, and the awareness that aging is inevitable for all of us. We both smiled adoringly at each other, grateful that we still have such precious time together." ~ Ama

SMILE

"Waking up this morning I smile.
Twenty-four brand new hours are before me."
Thich Nhat Hanh

Smiling is contagious and brings people together. Just think about how good you feel when you see the smiles on your grandchildren's faces. A smile can lighten a difficult situation, create a positive mood, lower stress and anxiety, and strengthen the immune system. Try these exercises, and see if you can bring more smiles into your life and the lives of your grandchildren:

✦ Wake up in the morning and, before you do anything, smile. See how this affects your outlook for the day.

✦ Smile when irritated or annoyed. This may be difficult, but it may change your mood.

✦ Smile at someone you don't know and notice the reaction. Do they smile back? How do you feel inside?

✦ In a "battle of wills" situation, which we all seem to experience, see if you can change thought patterns by adding a smile.

✦ Play a "don't you dare smile" game and see who cracks the first smile. Or play "wipe that smile off your face." Start with the youngest child and have him/her wipe the smile off his/her face, and pass it to the next person. Whoever keeps a straight face is the winner. It may be hard to stop the giggles.

"My four-year-old granddaughter, Larkin, loves to take treasure walks with me. We take a basket and walk together as we look for prized possessions, which include leaves of different colors and shapes, berries and seeds from plants, unusual rocks, bird feathers, and twigs. As these objects are placed in our basket, we talk about the shape, color and texture of each item. We use our imaginations and create stories about the things we find. We love to take off our shoes and feel the earth between our toes. Our walks are leisurely and fun, creating an enhanced awareness of our surroundings. Larkin and I never tire of this time together." ~ Grandma Sondra

"Each time our granddaughters come to visit, we walk to the park. It's our tradition to slowly walk along our make-believe 'Oingo-Boingo River,' which is a riverbed with no water, but has lots of twists, turns, and foliage throughout. We even take off our shoes and pretend we are walking in the imaginary river. Our girls love going on this adventure with us." ~ Granny Janni and Pops

WALK

"Walk as if you are kissing the Earth with your feet."
Thich Nhat Hanh

When we walk, we are usually not focusing on the physical act of walking; we just want to get there. Our minds are busy planning, worrying, or just thinking. However, if we really focus on just walking, the walking becomes a calming meditation that is more about the journey than the destination. Find a safe place to walk with your grandchildren, preferably one surrounded in beauty, and try this walking meditation:

Walk slowly.

Take a few steps with your eyes closed. (Be careful not to walk into a tree or fall into a ditch!)

Use your senses; what do you feel, hear, see, or smell?

Be aware of your legs and feet. Pay attention to each step.

Notice your feet touching the ground and transferring from one foot to the other. Is the ground soft? Wet? Cool? Warm?

Try smiling as you walk. What do you notice?

This is a pleasant way to take a time-out, calm everyone's over-occupied minds, and be in the present moment. Have some fun!

"My two granddaughters are close in age and I tend to do things with both of them together. When I come to visit, we always have a sleepover at my hotel. On my last trip, the older sister had a friend's birthday party to attend after breakfast. This meant her younger sister and I were able to spend another day and night together, something we don't often get to do. That night when we were lying in bed, she said (after making me promise not to tell anyone what she was going to tell me) that she was sad and didn't really have any friends. She talked and mostly I listened. I asked a few questions, and we thought about some things we could do to make it easier to invite a friend to go to the park after school one day. I know I cannot always 'make it all better' for them, but I can always be there to listen. I now realize how important it is for them to each have some alone time with Grancy." ~Grancy

LISTEN

"The word 'listen' contains the same letters
as the word 'silent.'"
Alfred Brendel

L istening is an invaluable skill that can be developed with practice. When you are with your grandchildren, pay close attention to what they say and encourage them to do the same with you. Deeper listening brings a richer experience. If you are not listening, you are not present.

⭐ Engage your grandchildren with this mealtime exercise:

⭐ Go around the table and give everybody two minutes to talk about something that happened during their day, without judgment or interruption. Ask the person sitting to their left to repeat what was just said. You will be surprised by what you learn.

⭐ Sit silently in a room and listen to the surrounding sounds. What do you hear—traffic, sirens, wind, people? What sounds do you hear inside your body—breathing, stomach growling, heart beating? This activity is great for any age.

⭐ Listen to one of your favorite songs and concentrate on the melody, the different instruments, the lyrics. Name the instruments and discuss the song's meaning. Older children will love this.

⭐ Play old-fashioned games, such as Simon Says and Telephone. See who is truly listening.

"I use a very different voice with my grandchildren, one that reflects my sheer inner joy at the privilege of speaking to my precious little ones. My husband has often commented that he wishes I used that voice on him! My grandkids know I am happy to be with them because I seem to have what my granddaughter, Harper, calls 'a smile in my voice.' That 'voice' changed the day I received an annoying message from my office and responded angrily in Harper's presence. When I got off the phone, she was in tears. I asked, 'What's wrong?' She answered, 'You were talking with a mean voice and that scared me.' It hurt my heart to know my words were okay, but my tone was frightening. A lesson learned, and yes, I will try to use 'that smiling voice' for the rest of my family." ~ Grandy

SPEAK MINDFULLY

"Six Points of Mindful Speech: Speak slowly, enunciate clearly, be concise, listen to yourself, listen to others, use silence as a part of speech."
Chogyam Trungpa

It's important to be aware of our words, as well as our tone and volume. When we speak to our grandchildren in a calm, nonjudgmental "inside voice," we are modeling how we would like them to speak to us and everyone else. It is not only what we say, but also how we say it, that makes an impact.

Play the "tone" game with your grandchildren. Say something nice in an angry voice. Say something not so nice in a sweet tone. Discuss how tone affects each one of us. How do they feel when someone speaks to them with a frustrated attitude?

Instead of raising your voice or speaking in an annoyed manner when your grandchildren tune you out, walk over to them, get on their level, look them in the eye, and mindfully reiterate your request.

When you are unhappy with the way your grandchildren speak to you, ask them to repeat their comments in a more respectful manner. Reinforce with positive feedback.

Do not monopolize a conversation. Silence and listening are powerful tools. Know when to speak up and when to hold back.

"About eight years ago my son, Aaron, his son, Eli, and I went to the park late at night to gaze at the stars and to view the Hale-Bopp Comet. It was very dark and very quiet. It was one of those exceptional moments where I could bond with my son and grandson without the extraneous distractions that usually mar that kind of special moment. Eli, then three years old, asked to look through the oversized binoculars. As he held the large binoculars to his eyes, without falling backward, he stood in silent amazement as he looked at the stars. All of a sudden, he yelled out, 'WOW! I SEE EARTH!' That was a magical moment that I will treasure forever." ~ Grandpa Ronnie

SEE

"If your eyes are opened, you'll see the things worth seeing."
Rumi

Children inspire us to notice so many of the things we take for granted. They have no agenda and are more grounded in the present moment, appreciating the dewdrops on the flowers, the sunrise over the mountaintop, a plane taking off, the waves in the ocean. Sharpen your personal vision lens by practicing the following activities with your grandchildren:

⭐ Pick three items and study them carefully for two minutes. Then put them away, and see how much you remember about each item. What did you really see? What was different about each item? What was the same? Older kids love this game.

⭐ Play I Spy, Find the Hidden Pictures, Where's Waldo? or Spot It.

⭐ Take a walk around the neighborhood and observe your surroundings with a fresh outlook. What new colors, shapes, textures, or objects do you discover?

⭐ Notice the clouds as they gather and float away. How many different formations can you find?

⭐ Look into the night sky and see who can find the most constellations.

"My grandkids call me 'Tata.' Since they were infants, it has been my pleasure to take them on long strolls. During these strolls, which now have evolved into walks, we appreciate nature—sounds, smells, colors, and textures. I have always believed that the olfactory sense is the gateway to neurological development. We sniff a lot of flowers, leaves, fruits, and vegetables. I love seeing their expressions when they smell a beautiful rose, honeysuckle, or rosemary. Because we always have classical music playing during our strolls, my nickname is now 'Sonata Tata.' Usually we do not have to do a lot of talking; just listening to music while we use our five senses is plenty." ~ Tata

SMELL

"Stop and smell the roses."
Unknown

The sense of smell is a gift that brings us into the here and now. When we smell the coffee, the freshly baked cookies, the freshly peeled tangerine, we become grounded in this sensual experience. We are aware and present. Smell sharpens our memory, elicits emotions, and alerts us to danger. With your grandchildren, try these activities for mindful sniffing:

Take a scent walk and notice the various fragrances. Are there especially wonderful smells? Unpleasant odors? Can you describe the smell?

Discuss your favorite smells. Is it Grandma's homemade applesauce or Grandpa's popcorn? Do feelings of comfort, security, and love surface, or not?

Play the "mystery scents" game. Put out three different items, such as lavender, mustard, and chocolate. Place a blindfold over each of your grandchildren's eyes, and ask them to guess each scent. Then, ask them questions: Do you like the smell? Do you want more or less of this smell? Does the smell remind you of anything?

"One of my favorite things to do is make French toast with my grandkids. Usually, it's a breakfast following a Shabbat dinner, so we take advantage of the leftover challah. It's not just the dip of the crispy, golden French toast morsels in the maple syrup (they call it 'dip dip') that we love but, as they say, the journey. It's the process. Watching my grandkids cracking the eggs into the bowl, never an easy task, has become a simple one. Also, the coordination of a three-year-old trying to stir the mixture with a fork is wonderful. And the kids accommodate me by allowing the addition of some vanilla or cinnamon in the mix. For them, adding candy sprinkles is the height of indulgence. Maybe it's just me projecting, as I myself start salivating; but I can tell their minds are in high gear as they anticipate the simple pleasure of tasting their first bite." ~ Grampy

TASTE

"Pay attention to each spoonful of food. As you bring it up to your mouth, use your mindfulness to be aware that this food is the gift of the whole universe."
Thich Nhat Hanh

Tasting food is an essential and satisfying experience. By paying attention to what we eat, we automatically slow down, increase digestion, and appreciate what we are consuming. Most of us are guilty of eating too fast as opposed to savoring each bite. Grandchildren and grandparents, slow down, chew more, and taste!

Next time you take your grandchildren for frozen yogurt or to the local farmer's market, ask them to select their favorite food. As they relish the first bite and their taste buds explode, ask them what they notice—is the flavor sweet, salty, bitter or sour?

Place three kinds of fruit or vegetables that look similar on a table, such as a peeled apple, a peeled pear, and a piece of jicama. Ask your grandchildren to taste each item. How do the flavors differ? Is there a variation in the textures?

Play a tasting game. Choose a food you and your grandchildren love, like pizza or pasta. As you begin to eat, slow down and pay attention to the taste. Does the flavor linger? Wear off after a few bites? Is the flavor just as you imagined?

"My thirteen-month-old granddaughter loves 'touch' books with the different fabrics and textures in them. We cuddle and read together, and I make exaggerated sounds as we touch the pages. In simple terms, I describe what I feel. I take her hand and say, 'Sooo soft, so scratchy, so smooth.' She loves to touch over and over again. Then, she does it on her own. And then, she puts her hand in mine and tells me to do it again. Touching delights her." ~ Nana

"Ever since my granddaughter was a baby, I have tickled her back, especially at bedtime. She loves it so much that, at the age of ten, the bedtime tickling is still the headliner every time she spends the night at our house or I babysit at her house. When she goes to college, will I still be tickling her back?" ~ LeaLea

TOUCH

"The things that matter most in our lives are not fantastic or grand. They are the moments when we touch one another."
Jack Kornfield

There is nothing more wonderful than cuddling with your grandchildren. It's soothing and loving. Touching is a direct way to connect.

Hug your grandchildren. Massage their feet. Tickle their backs. Rub noses. Do they like how this makes them feel? Talk about what feels good and what doesn't.

Play a sensory touch game with younger children. Put a variety of tactile objects into a basket, like a satin or velvet pillow, a furry stuffed animal, a cuddly blanket, slimy goop, feathers, or any sensory item you choose. Let everyone explore the different textures and sensations. Do they see the difference between touching vs. smelling vs. seeing?

Practice a "touching" meditation with older children. Ask them to feel the sensation of their feet in their shoes, feel their bottom and back as they're seated on a chair, and feel their clothes against their body. These are good exercises in teaching children to focus, center, and ground themselves in the present moment.

"While I try not to be a meddling grandma, it's hard for me to keep my mouth shut when it comes to the way my grandchildren eat. I am constantly reminding them to slow down and taste their food. The older one, in particular, loves dessert and will quickly stuff his face with the main meal so he can enjoy the sweets. One night, when I noticed everyone was inhaling the guacamole and chips, I suggested we have a 'chewing chip challenge.' The goal was to slow down our eating and see who could have the most chews for each chip. The kids loved this game and enjoyed each and every bite. Of course, I am still the annoying grandma who begs them to eat mindfully; but at least we are having some fun!" ~ Gram-cracker

MINDFULLY EAT

"Mindful eating is about awareness. When you eat mindfully, you slow down, pay attention to the food you're eating, and savor every bite."
Susan Albers

Many of us eat too fast and unconsciously overeat. We are distracted as we watch TV or read, stand at the kitchen counter, or eat on the go. Do you know that it takes twenty minutes for the brain to receive the "I am satisfied" signal? If we slow down and pay attention to what and how much we are eating, we can actually give our body a chance to catch up to our brain and receive the signal to eat the right amount. Mindful eating teaches us to savor each bite.

Try this. Eat a snack with your grandchild. Take time to really taste and enjoy the flavors. Put your fork down in between bites.

Do the "raisin exercise." Take one raisin (or a piece of chocolate or orange segment) and really look at it. Hold it up to the light and notice its surface. Put it up to your ear and hear it as you move it around with your fingers. Does a raisin have sound? What does a raisin smell like? Feel it with your hands. Is it soft, mushy, wrinkly? Put the raisin in your mouth, but do not swallow. Feel it on your lips, then your tongue. What are you noticing? Lastly, swallow the raisin.

Play the chewing game. Have everyone at the table pick a food they like and put a small bite into their mouths. See who can chew the longest without swallowing. Count your chews. The last one to swallow is the winner.

"Because of my work as a nutritionist and therapist, I've always preached to my kids and grandkids the benefit of checking in with their bodies to see whether they are hungry or full. My kids never took me seriously, but my three-year-old grandson takes my words of wisdom literally. For example, one day last year I took him to our favorite yogurt store. After finishing our treats, my grandson wanted more. I asked him, 'Isn't your tummy full?' He lifted up his shirt, looked down at his bare stomach, and laughingly asked, 'Tummy, what do you want?' Of course, his tummy answered back, 'More yogurt!' I loved this funny moment with him, and even now that he is older, we joke about how his tummy can talk to him." ~ Grand Mama

ACKNOWLEDGE HUNGER AND FULLNESS

"Eat when you are hungry. Stop when you are full.
Trust your body."
Geneen Roth

D o your grandchildren recognize the difference between an empty tummy and a full tummy? Do you? "My tummy is full; I will have some later" is a good concept for us to practice. We all can learn to listen to our bodies and know when we need to eat and when to stop.

Play the hunger scale game. It's a valuable tool to help understand conscious eating. Before eating your next meal or snack with your grandchildren, check inside your bodies and rate your hunger/fullness on a scale of 1 to 10:

10	= stuffed
8–9	= full
6-7	= satisfied
5	= neutral
3–4	= getting hungry
2	= really hungry
1	= starving

Practicing this exercise makes us more cognizant of our appetite.

Put down your fork in between bites and assess your fullness. This automatically slows down your eating pace and makes you more aware of your food choices and portion size.

"My granddaughter, Julia, had a sleepover at my house recently. She was having a hard time falling asleep at bedtime and asked me to lay down next to her. I asked her to close her eyes and picture the very top of her head opening up like a jar. I then told her to imagine me pouring a creamy milkshake inside. I slowly talked her through an imaginary journey of the milkshake flowing through each part of her face, then down her neck and shoulders, through her arms, and slowly continued through each part of her body. When we reached her toes, I looked over, and she was fast asleep!" ~ Bubbie

SCAN YOUR BODY

"Through repeated practice of the body scan over time,
we come to grasp the reality of our body as whole in the
present moment."
Jon Kabat-Zinn

Teach your grandchildren how to tune in to their bodies by practicing the body scan. As the kids move their attention from one body part to another, they learn to let go of distractions, and be more focused in the here and now. The added benefit is relaxation.

Invite your grandchildren to lie down in a comfortable place. As you name each body part, ask them to tune in to that particular area without moving it. Have them breathe in and out, as they bring their attention to each area. When their minds wander, and they will, gently bring the focus back to their bodies.

Older children can use the body scan independently, as a tool to calm down during stressful situations or before bed.

Depending on the age of the children, this meditation can last a few minutes, or as long as an hour.

"My eldest grandchild, a girl, now age eight, is tall and lean like her 6'6" father. She's always been a picky eater and doesn't care much about food. She loves to chew on ice; her dad jokes that she's always on the perfect supermodel diet. Last summer, she went to a day camp that was a forty-five-minute bus ride there and back. She would come home exhausted with her lunch not touched, and then complain of stomachaches and having a hard time going to the bathroom. My daughter decided it was time for a big discussion about self-care. She asked me to help, as sometimes it's easier to hear it from your grandma than your parents. So, my granddaughter and I sat down and had a long chat about the importance of fueling one's body so there's enough energy throughout the day. We talked about how the fiber in fruits and veggies moves food through the body, and the importance of having a colorful variety of nutrient-rich food at each meal. She half-listened and rolled her eyes, but I do see her trying to add more healthy choices into her diet." ~ Grandma

APPRECIATE YOUR BODY

"Look after your body or you will have nowhere else to live."
Jim Rohn

Our bodies are always with us, yet many of us are disconnected from them. It's important for children to respect and understand their physical selves, and to feel accepted and loved no matter what size or shape they are. Through our words and actions, we can show our grandchildren to value their bodies.

Comment on the amazing things our body does for us every day—eyes for seeing, arms for holding, legs for walking, ears for hearing, brains for thinking.

Discourage negative body talk about one's self and others.

Practice and model good hygiene, such as regular teeth brushing and bathing.

Encourage adequate rest, daily physical activity, and healthy eating.

Look at pictures and discuss unique body characteristics that apply to family members, such as height, bone structure, eye color, or skin tone.

"My husband and I were babysitting our three grandchildren for the weekend: Sophie, eight months; Avi, two; and Micah, four. Bedtime seems to be challenging for the two boys these days, so when it was time for bed they decided that they wanted to sleep with me, 'Granny.' Yes, I felt sorry for my husband that he wasn't selected, but I knew that he would get a better night's sleep than I would. I was right. Sleeping in the king-size bed with the two boys didn't work. They continuously jumped around and were way too talkative. I had a better idea. I told them that we would have an indoor 'camping trip.' I got sheets and laid them on the floor, and we tried to go to sleep. Again, no luck. I then moved in between them and told them that since we were 'camping,' we should try to imagine the stars in the sky and the sounds from outside; we had to be very quiet and not move! We held hands, took deep breaths, and imagined the beautiful (non-existent) sky and the chirping (non-existent) crickets. This seemed to calm them down. Once they were asleep, I slid out of our little campsite back to a normal bed. Sometime in the middle of the night, Avi decided to join me. He laid next to me, actually on top of me! When I woke in the morning, Micah was still sleeping in the tent, and Avi was playing with my hair. Did I sleep great that night? Not so much! But did I love this moment with my two little loves? Absolutely! By the way, Sophie slept blissfully in her crib!" ~ Granny

"There was never a child so lovely but his mother was glad to get him to sleep."
Ralph Waldo Emerson

Bedtime with grandchildren can be challenging! How many stalling techniques can one child create—more water, back rubbing, singing, reading, talking? To avoid bedtime struggles:

Keep nighttime routines consistent, whether at your home or theirs.

Read books, sing favorite bedtime songs, and massage bodies, but within a reasonable time frame.

Avoid overstimulation. Horsing around before bedtime is not a good idea.

Practice any breathing meditation that calms the mind and allows children to "let go" into sleep. The last section of this book provides some meditation exercises to try.

Cuddle!

EXPERIENCING THE
PRESENT MOMENT

"My fifteen-year-old grandson, Sam, is a fabulous athlete. Last year, he broke both his legs playing basketball. It was traumatic for him and the entire family. However, there was a silver lining because I ended up spending a lot of alone time with his younger sister, Emma, while Sam recovered in the hospital. Usually when I see my grandkids they are all together. This time Emma spent many nights with me alone, something she hadn't done before. We were able to have open meaningful conversations about her feelings and fears. She was very worried about her brother and what his recovery might entail. As I spent one-on-one time with Emma, I realized how much we both needed a place to express our emotions. We bonded over this and now have a more solid relationship. I realize how important it is to have alone time with each of my grandchildren, so they have the time, room, and freedom to express their deepest thoughts." ~ Grammy Beth

OBSERVE THOUGHTS, ANGER, AND WORRIES

"Don't believe every worried thought you have.
Worried thoughts are notoriously inaccurate."
Renee Jain

Thoughts can be scary and cumbersome, but pushing them away only makes matters worse. By explaining that thoughts are just thoughts, not necessarily reality, we can help our grandchildren learn to detach from their worries. Younger children may be scared of monsters, while older kids may be concerned about death, hurricanes, or fires. To change their relationship with fear and alter their anxiety, practice these exercises with grandchildren of any age:

FLOATING CLOUDS:
Ask the children to close their eyes and pay attention to their bothersome thoughts.

Then, imagine the thoughts floating by like clouds in the sky.

Watch as the thoughts drift away and disappear.

Discuss or draw any feelings that surface.

WORRY BOX:
Pay attention to scary thoughts or worries.

Write each one on a piece of paper.

Discuss what feelings arise.

Put the papers in a box and put the box away on a shelf.

Whenever worries surface, add to the box.

Make a yearly (or monthly) ceremony of throwing away the worries.

"I have been blessed to spend lots of wonderful and sometimes hair-raising time with my five grandchildren . . . separately, and in every imaginable combination. As my son-in-law's father used to say, 'Grandchildren are the reason we didn't kill our kids!' They're an undeniable gift. I have to say one moment stands above the rest. A few years ago my daughter was suffering from vertigo and I stayed with her for some time. On the first night, I put the kids to bed. Exhausted myself, I lay down next to my five-year-old granddaughter thinking I'd slip out as soon as she fell asleep. I don't know who fell asleep first, but with her dolls stabbing me in the back, I 'crashed.' I can't remember sleeping through the night in years, but I did that night. In the morning, I opened my eyes to see my beautiful, sweet, angelic granddaughter's back. As she turned and opened her eyes, she looked at me, smiled and said, 'Why would I EVER want to leave this cozy bed!'" ~ Mimi

FALL AWAKE

"Those who are awake live in a constant state of amazement."
Jack Kornfield

Children remind us to consciously awaken to all that is around us. They live with their eyes wide open. So often, we find ourselves on automatic pilot and do not see the world as they see it—with wonder and curiosity. Try these ideas, but no falling asleep allowed:

⭐ When you are with your grandchildren, set aside time to really be with them and appreciate the time together. Notice their expressions, moods, excitement, exhaustion, and behavior.

⭐ Concentrate on one thing at a time; no multitasking.

⭐ Turn off cell phones and focus.

⭐ If your mind wanders, bring it back and concentrate on what is happening now.

⭐ Time with grandchildren is special. Don't miss out!

"When my grandkids (ages one to seven) come to visit our house, one of the first things they do is run upstairs and open this huge closet filled with all their toys and games. I also have a meditation bell/bowl in this room because I teach and practice meditation. The older kids, especially, will stand on a chair and pull down the bell. I have taught them to hit the gong, close their eyes, and see how long they hear the sound. They think this is great fun and usually fight over who can be the one hitting the gong on the bowl." ~ Safta

LISTEN TO THE BELL

"Body, speech, and mind in perfect oneness,
I send my heart along with the sound of the bell.
May the hearers awaken from forgetfulness,
And transcend the path of anxiety and sorrow."
Thich Nhat Hanh

K ids love playing with bells. Let's invite mindfulness into our grandchildren's lives by teaching them that the sound of the bell is a reminder to stop what they are doing, pay attention to breathing, and be in the moment. Experiment with creative ways to use the bell:

Play "freeze." Ring the bell once. Everyone must completely stop what he/she is doing and focus inward. Whoever moves is out. Ring the bell again to unfreeze.

Close your eyes. Listen to the sound of the bell as it fades away. Raise your hand when you can no longer hear the tones. Younger kids love this game.

Use your smartphone to download free meditation bell apps and enjoy them with your grandchildren. Bowls— Tibetan Singing Bowls is a good option.

"One day last month we took our kids and grandkids to see a play. All six of us were squished into a three-row car, with my husband and grandson in the way back. Everyone was a little on edge as we rushed downtown to the theater. We had to make a stop to pick up something on the way, which required all of us to get out and then back into the car, and, of course, reset the seatbelts. My husband could not get his belt clicked in, and every time he tried, he undid my grandson's belt. My husband was getting impatient, my grandson was getting mad, and my son was huffing and puffing at both of them. Finally, I said, 'OK, everyone, let's take a moment to pause and take a deep breath.' Surprisingly, they listened to me and did this—one giant pause and then a deep inhale. And guess what? The seatbelts got hooked in, the tension was reduced, and off we went!" ~ Grammy

PAUSE . . . A . . . MOMENT (PAM)

*"Try pausing right before and after a new action.
Such pauses take a brief moment, yet they have the effect of
decompressing time and centering you."*
David Steindl-Rast

When you and your grandchildren get frustrated or overly emotional, use "PAM" to calm down and help everyone make better behavior choices. This acronym is self-explanatory:

- P: pause
- A: a
- M: moment

Practice this technique over and over. PAM really works.

"My grandchildren, nine and five respectively, think that Grandma 'KK' really is a mermaid because I would rather be in the water than on land. They have individually and collectively grown to adore and cherish our times together out on my paddleboard or surfboard. Together we spend quiet moments where the only sounds we focus on are those of the breeze gently gracing our faces, or the wonderful sounds of waves touching our boards. Brushing our toes in simple motions on the surface of the water has a soothing effect on our talks for long times together as we may sit on top of a board and just watch life around us. Creating a restful, peaceful, and gentle environment gives us the opportunity to have dialogue that takes us away from our landlocked routines. I know that both kids benefit from such a simple challenge as having the patience to wait for the perfect wave. They feel empowered and knowledgeable of their surroundings without anxiety, which gives them the encouragement to come and go paddleboarding or surfing, and to look for the beautiful creatures of the sea as we float together and explore. I want the kids to respect Mother Nature and the beauty of the ocean—which requires us to find a sense of calmness no matter what age. I hope when I am no longer around, they feel my presence and support when they teach their own children to 'hang ten.'" ~ KK

TAKE PLEASURE IN NATURE

"As I breathe in I can feel the fresh cool air filling my body.
I feel calm and relaxed.
I feel happy and safe on the earth."
Thich Nhat Hanh

Many of us take for granted the beauty of our natural surroundings, yet there is no better way to feel alive and centered than experiencing nature. Being outdoors inspires curiosity, improves concentration, stimulates imagination, and calms the mind. With your grandchildren:

Take a nature stroll and notice the smells, colors, textures, and sounds of everything you see.

Go camping. Sleep in tents and look at the stars.

Go to the beach—play on the sand and listen to the waves. Smell the ocean air.

Go to the mountains. Take a hike. Notice the birds, trees, wildlife, and insects.

Go to the park. Have a picnic on the grass. Look at the flowers and shrubs with renewed vision and awareness.

"Every year we go back East to celebrate Thanksgiving with our kids and grandkids. It has become a tradition to jump into a five foot leaf pile while we are all holding each other's hands, feeling the warmth and anticipation of the 3. . . 2 . . . 1 countdown . . . JUMP!! With the wonderful sounds of our laughter, we get buried under the crunchy, crispy, colorful, delicious-smelling leaves of autumn. This joyful activity brings a smile to our faces every time we think about it. Plus, we get the best family picture." ~ Nino and Poppy

"My granddaughter GG spent the night last weekend. We had so much fun. We always read *The Dumb Bunnies* and laugh out loud. We just like laughter. It calms us both and makes us content." ~ LaLa

LAUGH OUT LOUD

"You don't stop laughing because you grow old, you grow old because you stop laughing."
Michael Pritchard

No one likes to laugh more than children do—and thankfully, it's contagious. Laughing improves our mood, defuses a tense situation, calms the nervous system, and brings us into the present. When we lighten up, we feel more optimistic and positive. Connect and laugh with your grandchildren by:

- Playing games like Twister, Charades, or Pictionary

- Speaking in funny voices like Donald Duck or Bugs Bunny

- Doing a crazy walk or dance

- Sharing jokes

- Watching a funny movie

- Recounting humorous stories from the past

- Putting on a play and dressing up in creative costumes

- Being silly

"So, I'm driving my four-year-old granddaughter, Sloane, home from preschool, and I ask her what she did in school today, and she says, 'We goed to the park.' And I say, 'Not a word,' and she says, 'What?' And I say, 'Goed's not a word. It's went.' There's a slight pause from the back seat; then she says, 'And then we rided on the swings,' and I say, 'Not a word,' and she says, 'What?' And I say 'Rided's not a word. It's rode.' There's another pause from the back. Then Sloane says, 'You know what IS a word? Annoying.'" ~ Jay

ENJOY THE RIDE

"Life is a journey, not a destination."
Ralph Waldo Emerson

D riving grandchildren from place to place is one of the many responsibilities of grandparenting. This can be exhausting, challenging, and, at the same time, entertaining and informational. Remember, you have a captive audience. Take advantage of this time to joyfully connect and literally "enjoy the ride," not just in the car, but also in life.

⭐ Play games such as Twenty Questions, Travel Bingo, the License Plate Game, or "I'm going on a picnic."

⭐ Count convertibles, name types of trucks, read billboards and signs, spot colors.

⭐ Sing songs. Listen to audiobooks and podcasts.

⭐ See who can be the quietest for the longest.

⭐ Tell stories, chat and catch up with each other.

⭐ And listen.

"I have been a yoga teacher for over twenty years and now a grammy to my four-year-old granddaughter, Hazel. Through my long yoga journey, I have learned powerful values that are the perfect grandma training ground—kindness, curiosity, perseverance, and laughter. Hazel and I can be sitting on the grass taking three deep calming breaths together, pretending we are fierce lions, or simply singing a song. We have had so many of what I would call 'yogic moments' of loving connection. One of my most vivid memories is attending a 'Mommy and Me' class when Hazel was three months old. We began the class by placing the babies on their backs, gazing into their eyes, opening their arms on the inhale and bringing their hands back to their bellies on the exhale. Hazel rolled over onto her belly (an accomplishment at this stage), positioned herself on her forearms, mimicking cobra, and took a very slow, curious scan of the room and cooed her approval. I remember feeling so grateful to be sharing this moment with her. The other day, I saw a T-shirt that says it all: 'Never underestimate the power of a grandma that loves yoga.'" ~ Grammy

PRACTICE YOGA

"Yoga is the stilling of the fluctuations of the mind."
Patanjali

A wonderful way to help our grandchildren move their bodies, access their breath, and center themselves is by doing yoga poses with them. Yoga builds self-respect, develops focus and concentration, and increases the mind-body connection. No matter what age, children love getting on the floor and moving. Practice these fun poses together:

SUN SALUTATION: Inhale as you raise both hands to the sky and welcome the day. Exhale as you bring both arms to your sides.

CAT-COW: Inhale, arch your back like a cat, and tuck in your chin. Exhale, gently look up, and drop your spine.

BUTTERFLY: Sit with the soles of your feet together. Flap your legs slowly like butterfly wings. Keep your shoulders back. Breathe in and out.

CHILD'S POSE: Kneel on the floor and sit on your heels. Fold your torso over your thighs and put your forehead to the floor. Your hands can be by your sides or above your head on the floor. Rest and breathe.

MEDITATIONS

CALM YOURSELF

"You can't calm the storm, so stop trying. What you CAN do is calm yourself; the storm will pass."
Timber Hawkeye

In the mindfulness tradition, the repetition of a positive mantra builds compassion and reduces anxiety, stress, and anger. The following "metta"—or loving-kindness— meditations are especially calming:

⭐ Get into a comfortable position. Close your eyes. Notice your breath. Check in with your inner feelings and repeat the words: "May I have inner peace. May I be emotionally strong. May I live with ease." Or make up a different mantra that will soothe you.

⭐ If you are concerned about someone other than yourself, the following mantra can be chanted: "May she be healthy. May she be safe. May she be free of stress." Again, substitute whatever wording works best for your particular situation.

S...T...O...P...MEDITATION

"Dwelling in the present moment,
I know this is a wonderful moment."
Thich Nhat Hanh

This "mini" meditation, using the acronym *STOP*, is an effective tool to help you and your grandchildren slow down and be cognizant of your surroundings. Say each letter and its definition aloud:

- S: stop what you are doing.
- T: take a deep breath.
- O: observe what is going on now.
- P: proceed with renewed clarity.

Practice this exercise so when you say "STOP" everyone knows the drill and is transported into the present moment. Older children find this technique especially grounding.

ANCHOR MEDITATION

"Feelings come and go like clouds in a windy sky.
Conscious breathing is my anchor."
Thich Nhat Hanh

While it is not easy to rein in a wandering mind, the breath is there to support us. It is our friend, is easily accessible, regulates our bodies, and connects us to the here and now. Learn to appreciate the unique power of the breath by rehearsing this visualization exercise together with your grandchildren:

Describe and discuss how an anchor stabilizes a ship.

Close your eyes and picture a ship anchored to the bottom of the ocean.

Explain how the breath is the anchor for our minds. As we breathe, we become calmer and steadier, just like a ship.

For younger children, increase their understanding of this metaphor by either displaying pictures of ships and anchors, or encouraging them to draw their own creative version.

SQUARE BREATHING/BELLY BREATHING

"Breathing in, I calm my body.
Breathing out, I smile."
Thich Nhat Hanh

Our breath anchors us to the present moment and calms the nervous system. Try one of these breathing techniques with your grandchildren, especially when there is a meltdown. You will both benefit.

FOR OLDER CHILDREN, PRACTICE SQUARE BREATHING:
Begin by visualizing a square and focusing on the bottom left-hand corner. As your mind travels up the left side, inhale and count to four. Hold your breath for four counts as you envision the top line of the square. Then exhale, counting 1, 2, 3, 4, as your mind travels down the right side of the square. Hold your breath again for four counts as you move across the bottom to complete the square. Repeat four times and notice your body relax.

FOR YOUNGER CHILDREN, TRY BELLY BREATHING:
Have your grandchildren put one hand on their belly and one on their heart. Ask them to breathe and feel their stomach expand and contract. Repeat at least four times.

BREATHE WITH THE BEAR

"Teddy bears don't need hearts
as they are already stuffed with love."
Unknown

Since most kids love stuffed animals, inspire your grandchildren to focus on their breathing by using a teddy bear, or any favorite stuffie or doll, as a prop:

⭐ Ask your grandchildren to lie on the floor.

⭐ Place a teddy bear on each of their bellies and watch them become aware of the bear rising and falling in sync with their own breath.

⭐ Spark your grandchildren's interest by making this a game. What happens to the teddy bear as they breathe faster? Slower? Does the bear fall off?

⭐ What do they notice happening in their body? Do they feel calmer or do they feel sleepy? What else?

Watch their enthusiasm as they learn to pay attention to their breathing, and see that this exercise really can help them refocus and calm their inner feelings.

Leslie's Story

Growing up in Texas as the rabbi's daughter had its perks, and its downsides. Even though I felt as if I lived in a fishbowl, I am not sure that was the reality. But I did know there were plenty of eyes on me. So much so that I was too worried about how I appeared from the outside, and did not concentrate on how I felt on the inside. My husband, Michael, helped me find a clearer pathway. Spirituality and faith have always been in my blood, but I buried my innermost feelings until I was in my early thirties and became a mom. Being married, having children, and realizing the immense responsibility mixed with the total joy and overflowing love, made me pay attention to who I was and wanted to be. I began discovering me, and my inner soul began to flourish.

The years have rapidly passed, and my two glorious sons are adults, and now my husband and I are doting grandparents. As we took on this new role, we realized we needed to learn more about being "grandparents." After all, it had been years since we parented young children, and much has changed. Forget about all the new fancy strollers and car seats and high chairs. Most importantly, there are different parenting guidelines. Technology has invaded our lives, and every day, there is something new to discover and learn. Not only that, but how do I/we effectively and lovingly relate to our own children in their roles as parents?

Grandparenting to me is a whole new ball game. If I am looking to educate myself as a vital, enthusiastic, understanding and loving grandparent, aren't others in my position feeling the same way? With this in mind, my dear friend and fellow new grandparent Kay Ziplow and I became partners, creating the website GrandparentsLink.com

I had no idea what kind of commitment, research, and time would be necessary to create a site. The workload has been daunting, and GrandparentsLink.com has proven to be a spiritual, technological, and educational adventure. As Kay and I realized we needed valuable and relatable content for our site, I asked my close friend and grandparent Pam Siegel to write an article for us. Pam is a therapist specializing in mindfulness. Her thought-provoking and stimulating article on "mindful grandparenting" opened a whole new world to me and to our GrandparentsLink.com's viewers. It was at this point that Pam and I decided we wanted to impart our grandparent mindfulness in a more extended format that grandparents could learn to use in their daily lives.

Pam's Story

As part of my continuing education for my psychotherapy practice, I began an intensive course on mindfulness practice with Jerome Front. His teachings and inspiration significantly changed my life. I knew very little about mindfulness at the time but saw that many therapists were beginning to use it with their clients. Mindfulness encourages being in the present moment, self-reflection, non-judgment, and awareness. During the course, I was also planning my daughter's wedding, and I got to experience firsthand the powerful benefits of this way of being. Mindfulness taught me to enjoy the daily process of planning the wedding rather than focusing on the one "big day." What could have been tense, goal-oriented, mindless work for my daughter and me was fun, fulfilling, and bonding. The wedding day was perfect, but I can honestly say that the time leading up to it was even better.

Since then, I have become immersed in the growing field of mindfulness. I see how it has positively affected my personal and professional life. It has helped many of my clients with a variety of disorders and impacted my reactions to people and difficult situations. So, in 2011, when I was blessed with the birth of two grandchildren, I was already thinking about being a very present grandparent. Many of my friends and family who were already grandparents told me of the uniqueness of these relationships. However, it wasn't until my husband, Lenny, and I experienced grandparenting firsthand that I fully understood how deep my feelings would be for these new additions in my life.

When Leslie asked me to write an article for GrandparentsLink.com on being a grandparent, I reflected on why these two (now five) little people have had such an amazing impact on me. I know that I was a devoted mother to my two children and loved them deeply, but there is something in the grandparent–grandchild relationship that feels different. Of course, the reasons many grandparents love grandparenting are certainly part of the story. However, for me, the bigger influence on the relationships with my now five grandchildren is mindfulness. I have a daily morning meditation practice that helps me set an intention of how I want to interact in my life, especially with these young little people. I routinely practice yoga and lead a mindfulness support group, both activities that reinforce the principles of mindfulness.

When I raised my own children I took pride in the fact that I could multitask and juggle many different activities with them. Today I am very different. I am careful to spend quality time with my grandchildren, putting away distractions and focusing on one thing at a time. I constantly meditate on ways to let go of things that bother me and accept certain situations that are not perfect. While I certainly am not mindful all the time, I am now at least aware when I am not being mindful, something that never crossed my mind before this training.

Spending time with my grandchildren is my favorite activity. I love their fresh, uninhibited, nonjudgmental view of the world, something that has opened my mind and sparked my curiosity about such things as trucks, diggers, clouds, and the moon. My husband and I have learned so much hanging out with our brood of grandkids. All of these feelings and realizations were the inspiration for this book.

ACKNOWLEDGMENTS

This book has certainly been a labor of love. There are many people who have supported us throughout this long journey.

Thank you to Jan Lasky Platt, who brought us together in friendship. She will always be in our hearts.

We are indebted to the multi-talented Amy L. Siegel—computer expert, editor, attorney, friend, and number one supporter. No matter how busy Amy was, she always responded to our cries for help.

Heartfelt thanks to Jerome Front, LMFT, who first introduced mindfulness to us years ago and who believed in our book from the beginning.

A big hug to the ever-patient Kimberley Cameron, who continually mentored us throughout this process.

A special thanks to our wonderful grandparent friends who willingly contributed their warm and poignant stories, making our book so much more special: Fran, Mindy, Joe, Barbara, Irwin, Reveta, Donna, Arlene, Randi, Bob, Ron, Sandy, Edna, Bobby, Rachel, Jay, Gail, Susan, Lenny, Michael, Lonnie, Laurie, Marlene, Cindy, Sondra, Janni, Mark, Nancy, Ronnie, Rhonda, Janet, Beth, Nancy W., Kay, Karen, Ken, Mary, Gayle, and Jane.

Thank you to the entire Koehler Publishing team: John, Joe, Kellie, Hannah, and Skyler. This wouldn't have happened without their expertise and guidance.

Kudos to Shari Stauch, our enthusiastic and energetic marketer, and to talented website designer Danielle Koehler.

And again a special thank-you to our extra-wonderful husbands, Lenny and Michael, for their guidance, input, patience, and love.

Last but not least, we thank our incredible grandchildren, Dylan, Lily, Ethan, Jack, Asher, Spencer, and Gavin. They are the inspiration for this book, and our love for them continues to motivate us to grow and be more present in our own lives.

PERMISSION TO QUOTE

"The greatest gift we can make to others is our true presence."
Thich Nhat Hanh; reprinted from *Teachings On Love* (1998, 2007) by Thich Nhat Hanh with permission of Parallax Press, www.parallax.org, November 2017.

"In the beginner's mind there are many possibilities, but in the expert's there are few."
Shunryu Suzuki; permission granted by San Francisco Zen Center, August 2017.

"Slow down, calm down, don't worry, don't hurry, trust the process."
Alexandra Stoddard; permission granted by Alexandra Stoddard, September 2017.

"Focus on one thing at a time. Enjoy it, taking the most pleasant memories of it into the next experience."
Unknown

"I've learned that whenever I decide to trust something with an open heart, I usually make the right decision."
Maya Angelou; permission granted by Caged Bird Legacy LLC, June 2019.

"If you judge people, you have no time to love them."
Mother Teresa; permission granted by Mother Teresa Center, June 2019.

"A moment of patience, in a moment of anger, saves a thousand moments of regret."
Unknown

"You can grow ideas in the garden of your mind."
Fred Rogers; permission granted by the Fred Rogers Company,
June 2019.

"Learning to let go, this is the secret to happiness."
Buddha

"When you set an intention, when you commit, the entire universe conspires to make it happen."
Sandy Forster, founder of www.wildlyweathywomen.com; permission granted by Sandy Forster, August 2017.

"Finally I am coming to the conclusion that my highest ambition is to be what I already am."
Thomas Merton, from his Journal of Thomas Merton Series, October 2, 1958; permission granted by Thomas Merton Center, August 2017.

"Live, laugh, love."
Unknown

"We have only now, only this single eternal moment opening and unfolding before us, day and night."
Jack Kornfield; permission granted by Jack Kornfield, October 2017.

"It is not what technology does to us, it is what we do to technology. Get smart with technology, choose wisely and use it in a way that benefits both you and those around you."
Headspace.com; permission granted by Headspace, August 2017.

"The single greatest thing you can do to change your life today would be to start being grateful for what you have right now. And the more grateful you are, the more you get."
Oprah Winfrey; permission granted by Material Courtesy of Harpo, Inc., October 2017.

"The greatest work that kindness does to others is that it makes them kind themselves."
Amelia Earhart; permission granted by CMG Worldwide, September 2017.

"Respond from the center of the hurricane, rather than reacting from the chaos of a storm."
George Mumford; reprinted from *The Mindful Athlete: Secrets to Pure Performance* (2015) with permission of Parallax Press, www.parallax.org, September 2017.

"Education today needs not only to develop intelligence, but also to support basic human values of warm-heartedness and compassion."
Dalai Lama XIV; from His Holiness's Twitter page, November 2017.

"The moment you accept what troubles you've been given, the door will open."
Rumi

"Silence is the sleep that nourishes wisdom."
Francis Bacon

"Remembering a wrong is like carrying a burden on the mind."
Buddha

"Today you are you! That is truer than true! There is no one alive who is you-er than you!"
Dr. Seuss; permission granted by Dr. Seuss Enterprises, LP, 2019.

"We can complain because rose bushes have thorns, or rejoice because thorn bushes have roses."
Abraham Lincoln

"Children are natural mimics who act like their parents despite every effort to teach them good manners."
Unknown

"The willingness to accept responsibility for one's own life is the source from which self-respect springs."
Joan Didion; excerpt from "On Self-Respect," copyright 1961 by Joan Didion; originally published in *Vogue Magazine* 1961, reprinted in *Slouching Towards Bethlehem*; quote reprinted by permission of the author. November 2017.

"Life is what happens when your cell phone is charging."
Unknown

"I hold the Earth and the Sky with love in my heart. I hold the Oceans and Rivers with love in my heart. I hold the creatures of the Earth with love in my heart. Beings big or small, near or far, living now, or to come. May they be happy, May they be safe, And may their hearts be filled with joy."
Joseph Emet; permission granted by Joseph Emet, July 2017.

"Waking up this morning I smile. Twenty-four brand new hours are before me."
Thich Nhat Hanh; reprinted from *Planting Seeds: Practicing Mindfulness with Children* by Thich Nhat Hanh and Plum Village Community (2011) with permission of Parallax Press, www.parallax.org, November 2017.

"Walk as if you are kissing the Earth with your feet."
Thich Nhat Hanh; reprinted from *The Long Road Turns to Joy* by Thich Nhat Hanh (1996, 2011), Parallax Press, www.parallax.org, August 2017.

"The word 'listen' contains the same letters as the word 'silent.'"
Alfred Brendel; permission granted by Alfred Brendel, July 2017.

"Six Points of Mindful Speech: Speak slowly, enunciate clearly, be concise, listen to yourself, listen to others, use silence as a part of speech."
Chogyam Trungpa; permission granted by Chogyam Trungpa, September 2017.

"If your eyes are opened, you'll see the things worth seeing."
Rumi

"Stop and smell the roses."
Unknown

"Pay attention to each spoonful of food. As you bring it up to your mouth, use your mindfulness to be aware that this food is the gift of the whole universe."
Thich Nhat Hanh; reprinted from *How to Eat* (2014) by Thich Nhat Hanh, Parallax Press, www.parallax.org, September 2017.

"The things that matter most in our lives are not fantastic or grand. They are the moments when we touch one another."
Jack Kornfield; permission granted by Jack Kornfield, July 2017.

"Mindful eating is about awareness. When you eat mindfully, you slow down, pay attention to the food you're eating, and savor every bite."
Dr. Susan Albers; permission granted by Dr. Susan Albers, December 2017.

"Eat when you are hungry. Stop when you are full. Trust your body."
Geneen Roth; permission granted by Geneen Roth, August 2017.

"Through repeated practice of the body scan over time, we come to grasp the reality of our body as whole in the present moment."
Jon Kabat-Zinn; Excerpts from *Full Catastrophe Living* by Jon Kabat-Zinn, copyright © 1990 by Jon Kabat-Zinn. Used by permission of Dell Publishing, an imprint of Random House, a division of Penguin Random House LLC. All rights reserved.

"Take care of your body. It's the only place you have to live."
Jim Rohn, America's foremost business philosopher; reprinted with permission from Success©2016, www.SUCCESS.COM

"There was never a child so lovely but his mother was glad to get him to sleep."
Ralph Waldo Emerson

"Don't believe every worried thought you have. Worried thoughts are notoriously inaccurate."
Renee Jain; permission granted by Renee Jain, July 2017.

"Those who are awake live in a constant state of amazement."
Jack Kornfield; permission granted by Jack Kornfield, October 2017.

"Body, speech, and mind in perfect oneness,
I send my heart along with the sound of the bell.
May the hearers awaken from forgetfulness
And transcend the path of anxiety and sorrow."
Thich Nhat Hanh; reprinted from *Present Moment, Wonderful Moment: Mindfulness Verses for Daily Living* (1990, 2007) by Thich Nhat Hanh, with permission of Parallax Press, Berkeley, California, www.parallax.org, August 2017.

"Try pausing right before and after a new action. Such pauses take a brief moment, yet they have the effect of decompressing time and centering you."
David Steindl-Rast; permission granted by Br. David Steindl-Rast, Gratefulness.org, August 2017.

"As I breathe in I can feel the fresh cool air filling my body.
I feel calm and relaxed.
I feel happy and safe on the earth."
Thich Nhat Hanh; reprinted from *Present Moment, Wonderful Moment* (1990, 2007) by Thich Nhat Hanh, Parallax Press www.parallax.org November 2017

"You don't stop laughing because you grow old, you grow old because you stop laughing."
Michael Pritchard; permission granted by Michael Pritchard, August 2017.

"Life is a journey, not a destination."
Ralph Waldo Emerson

"Yoga is the stilling of the fluctuations of the mind."
Patanjali

"You can't calm the storm, so stop trying. What you CAN do is calm yourself; the storm will pass."
Timber Hawkeye; permission granted by Timber Hawkeye, October 2017.

"Dwelling in the present moment, I know this is a wonderful moment."
Thich Nhat Hanh; reprinted from *Present Moment, Wonderful Moment: Mindfulness Verses for Daily Living* (1990, 2007) by Thich Nhat Hanh, with permission of Parallax Press, Berkeley, California, www.parallax.org, August 2017.

"Feelings come and go like clouds in a windy sky. Conscious breathing is my anchor."
Thich Nhat Hanh; reprinted from *Present Moment, Wonderful Moment: Mindfulness Verses for Daily Living* (1990, 2007) by Thich Nhat Hanh with permission of Parallax Press, Berkeley, California, www.parallax.org, August 2017.

"Breathing in, I calm my body. Breathing out, I smile."
Thich Nhat Hanh; reprinted from *Present Moment, Wonderful Moment: Mindfulness Verses for Daily Living* (1990, 2007) by Thich Nhat Hanh, with permission of Parallax Press, Berkeley, California, www.parallax.org, August 2017.

"Teddy bears don't need hearts as they are already stuffed with love."
Unknown

WHO'S WHO

ABRAHAM LINCOLN
American statesman and lawyer who served as sixteenth president of the United States

ALEXANDRA STODDARD
Author, interior designer, and lifestyle philosopher

ALFRED BRENDEL
Austrian pianist, poet, and author

AMELIA EARHART
American aviation pioneer and author; first female to fly solo across the Atlantic Ocean

BUDDHA
Sage on whose teachings Buddhism was founded

CHOGYAM TRUNGPA
Meditation master, teacher, and artist; founded first Buddhist-inspired university in Colorado

DALAI LAMA XIV
Current spiritual leader of the Tibetan people, Tenzin Gyatso

DAVID STEINDL-RAST
Catholic Benedictine monk and author

DR. SEUSS
Theodor Seuss Geisel; American writer and cartoonist widely known for his children's books, which he wrote and illustrated

FRANCIS BACON
English philosopher, statesman, scientist, jurist, orator, and author

GENEEN ROTH
Well-known author of numerous books on how to have a healthy relationship with food, such as *Women, Food, and God*

GEORGE MUMFORD
Public speaker and mindfulness coach; wrote *The Mindful Athlete*

GEORGE ORWELL
Pen name for Eric Blair; English novelist, essayist, journalist, and critic who is known for his books *1984* and *Animal House*

HEADSPACE.COM
A comprehensive online resource and mobile app service

JACK KORNFIELD
Leading American Buddhist teacher who trained as a Buddhist monk and introduced mindfulness and Vipassana meditation to the West

JEROME FRONT
A mindfulness teacher; licensed psychotherapist who has taught mindfulness classes, workshops, and retreats since 1993

JIM ROHN
American entrepreneur, author, and motivational speaker

JOAN DIDION
American author, essayist, and journalist

JON KABAT-ZINN
A professor of medicine emeritus, founder of MBSR program at University of Massachusetts, scientist, meditation teacher, author; responsible for bringing mindfulness to mainstream medicine and society

JOSEPH EMET
Started the Mindfulness Meditation Centre in 1997 and author of *Buddha's Book of Sleep*

MAYA ANGELOU
American poet, memoirist, and civil rights activist

MICHAEL PRITCHARD
American stand-up comedian, youth counselor, speaker, and advocate of social emotional learning.

MOTHER TERESA
Roman Catholic religious sister and missionary who lived in India and was known for her charitable work

MR. ROGERS
Fred Rogers; American educator, Presbyterian minister, songwriter, author, and television host

OPRAH WINFREY
American media proprietor, talk-show host, actress, producer, and philanthropist

PATANJALI
One of many people with this Sanskrit name who contributed to writing the Yoga Sutras

RALPH WALDO EMERSON
American essayist, lecturer, and poet best known for his essays entitled "Self-Reliance"

RENEE JAIN
Respected childhood happiness and resilience expert

RUMI
Thirteenth-century Persian poet, scholar, and theologian

SANDY FORSTER
International speaker and best-selling author

SHUNRYU SUZUKI
Soto Zen monk and teacher; author of *Zen Mind, Beginner's Mind*

SUSAN ALBERS
Licensed clinical psychologist and author specializing in eating issues, body image concerns, and mindfulness

THICH NHAT HAHN
Vietnamese Zen Buddhist monk, global spiritual teacher, author, poet and peace activist

THOMAS MERTON
Well-known American Catholic writer and mystic; a Trappist monk who wrote over sixty books

TIMBER HAWKEYE
Speaker and author of *Buddhist Boot Camp* and memoir *Faithfully Religionless*

REFERENCES

Alidina, Shamash. 2010. *Mindfulness for Dummies*. West Sussex, England. Wiley and Sons.

Brantley, Jeffrey and Wendy Millstine. 2009. *Five Good Minutes in Your Body*. Oakland, California. New Harbinger Publications.

Germer, Christopher. 2009. *The Mindful Path to Self-Compassion*. New York, New York. Guilford Press.

Greenland, Susan Kaiser. 2010. *The Mindful Child*. New York, New York. Atria.

Hanson, Rick. *Just One Thing*. 2011. Oakland, California. New Harbinger Publications.

Kabat-Zinn, Myla, and Jon Kabat-Zinn. 1997. *Everyday Blessings*. New York, New York. Hyperion

Kabat-Zinn, Jon. 1990. *Full Catastrophe Living*. New York, New York. Random House.

Kabat-Zinn, Jon. 2012. *Mindfulness for Beginners*. Boulder, Colorado. Sounds True, Inc.

Kabat-Zinn, Jon. 2007. *Arriving at your Own Door*. New York, New York. Hyperion.

Maclean, Kerry Lee. 2009. *Moody Cow Meditates*. Boston, Massachusetts. Wisdom Publications.

Maclean, Kerry Lee. 2004. *Peaceful Piggy Meditation*. Chicago, Illinois. Albert Whitman and Co.

Marlowe, Sara. 2013. *No Ordinary Apple*. Somerville, Massachusetts. Wisdom Publications.

Paston, Bryna Nelson. 2010. *How to Be A Perfect Grandma*. Naperville, Illinois.

Snel, Eline. 2013. *Sitting Still Like a Frog*. Boston, Massachusetts. Shambhala Publications.

Somov, Pavel G. 2008. *Eating the Moment*. Oakland, California. New Harbinger Publications.

Stahl, Bob, and Elisha Goldstein. 2010. *Mindfulness Based Stress Reduction Workbook*. Oakland, Ca. New Harbinger Publications.

Thich Nhat Hanh. 2012. *A Handful of Quiet*. Berkley, California. Plum Blossom Books.

Thich Nhat Hanh. 2011. *Planting Seeds: Practicing Mindfulness with Children*. Berkley, California. Parallax Press.

Thich Nhat Hanh. 1975. *The Miracle of Mindfulness*. Boston. Beacon Press.

Willard, Christopher. 2010. *Child's Mind*. Berkley, California. Parallax Press.

PAM SIEGEL MPH, MFT is a licensed marriage family therapist in private practice in West Los Angeles. She has a master's in health education from UCLA and an additional master's in counseling from California State University, Northridge. She is a certified mindfulness therapist and implements meditation and other mindfulness tools to help her clients with a variety of issues. For over twelve years, Pam has led a weekly mindfulness support group. She is actively involved in the mindfulness and yoga community and has her own daily practice and website, www.pamsiegel.com. Pam is a member of the California Association of Marriage Family Therapists.

LESLIE ZINBERG has a BS in elementary education from the University of Texas at Austin, and has co-written two successful parenting books, *The Pink and Blue Baby Pages*, written in 1995, and *The Pink and Blue Toddler Pages*, written in 1999. Both books were featured in national publicity campaigns, with appearances on the *Today Show*, QVC, and local television and radio segments across the country. Leslie is the cofounder of the grandparent website, www.grandparentslink.com.

Visit www.grandparentingrenewreliverejoice.com for more information and resources.

CPSIA information can be obtained
at www.ICGtesting.com
Printed in the USA
JSHW020839291119
2686JS00003B/18